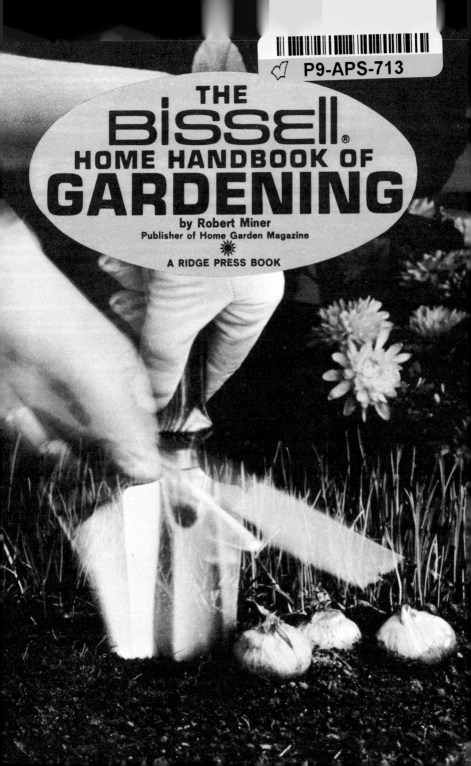

THE BiSSELL
HOME HANDBOOK OF
GARDENING

by Robert Miner
Publisher of Home Garden Magazine

A RIDGE PRESS BOOK

CONTENTS

1
**WHAT
IS A
GARDEN?**
PAGE 6

4
**LAWN MAKIN
AND
MAINTENANC**
PAGE 30

7
VEGETABLES
PAGE 70

10
TOOLS
PAGE 102

Line drawings by Harry Rosenbaum

PHOTO CREDITS
W. Atlee Burpee Co., pages 52-53
M. Glanzman, pages 20-21
Gottscho-Schleisner, Inc., pages 28-29,
44-45, 76-77, 92-93; Hampfler, pages 4-5
Monkmeyer, pages 12-13, 108-109, 116-117
R. Stahman, pages 100-101
John Stewart, pages 68-69

2
PLANNING AND LANDSCAPING
PAGE 14

3
SOIL MANAGEMENT
PAGE 22

5
SHRUBS AND VINES
PAGE 46

6
THE FLOWER GARDEN
PAGE 54

8
TREES
PAGE 78

9
PRUNING
PAGE 94

11
PEST CONTROL
PAGE 110

GARDENING QUESTIONS AND ANSWERS
PAGE 118

INDEX, PAGE 126

1

WHAT IS A GARDEN?

Not a squared-off plot in
which plants grow in
regimented rows, but rather
all that contributes to
the whole outdoor picture—that
is what a garden should be

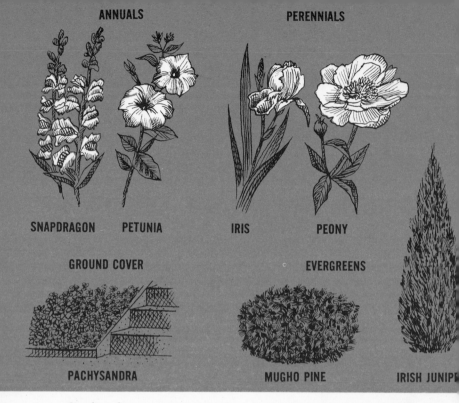

ANNUALS

SNAPDRAGON   PETUNIA

PERENNIALS

IRIS   PEONY

GROUND COVER

PACHYSANDRA

EVERGREENS

MUGHO PINE   IRISH JUNIPE

Garden pleasure comes from knowing and using a variety of plant forms. Each one illustrated has its own distinct design advantage

Do you want a truly beautiful garden, but aren't sure where or when to start? Or, like so many city and suburban homeowners, do you simply want to get the place looking decent before you desert to the golf course or to your new boat? Either way, this book is meant for you.

The elaborate gardens at one time pictured in the glossier of the gardening magazines represented the devoted efforts of highly trained and sometimes prohibitively expensive professionals. These were the gardens that too often turned the home owner away from the idea of a garden.

Even the commercial rose growers have sometimes been guilty of making the hobby of gardening seem too overwhelming an undertaking. One grower has remarked that he and his competitors probably scare more people away from rose-growing than they introduce to this fascinating activity. How? By the instructions that they send out with each rose bush.

"How to plant" instructions sometimes run three pages in small type. Bug and disease treatment, along with pruning information, complete the advice to the purchaser. Taken all together it would seem to require a graduate degree in horticulture to raise a rose bush, when all that really is necessary is to dig a hole, stick the rose plant in, and fill in the soil.

Gardening is the simplest pastime we know. The truth is, you don't need a book at all, just the basic courage to buy some plants and dig holes for them. Your own experience will show you, as these plants mature, bloom, shed for the winter, and come forth again the next spring, what the growth of plants is like. Ways to improve the appearance, the health, and the bloom of the plants will suggest themselves to you. You will find this plant watching a fascinating experience.

In that case, why are we writing this book? It is hoped that reading these pages will save a gardener—new or old—time and effort right from the start. By suggesting ways of achieving initial success in design, in planting, and in care, this book will have contributed to the rich pleasures to be found in successful gardening.

What is a garden? It might be a good idea to think about

this before deciding what kind of garden you want. To some, a garden means a single plot of ground, cultivated in rows, and composed of vegetables or of flowering plants. To others, it is the entire landscape—lawn, trees, flowers. Throughout this book, the garden we will be talking about is the complete garden—all of the area which surrounds and complements the house. Our garden includes all the lawn and all the trees, the flowering plants of all kinds, and specialties such as vegetables, vines, and terrace tub plants. It includes paths on which to walk, benches on which to sit, and features such as pools, statuary, arbors, and bird feeders, which complete its personality and provide an environment in which man and nature meet happily.

Plants make the garden, and their total number in any one garden can reach into the thousands. While some plants are grown mostly for their form and foliage, others are grown for bloom or fruit, for fall color, for ground cover, for shade, or for screening. Regardless of the purpose, all plants share the same general process of growth and the same range of requirements in terms of air, water, sun, and food. However, the variations within the range of these needs are many.

Plant Language Contains Two Vocabularies. One is composed of "common" names, as in the words "maple" and "crab apple." Most gardeners use the common vocabulary when naming a plant. In general, it is the easiest way to identify plants at the nursery when you are making a purchase. The more exact nomenclature has been developed through hundreds of years of botanical research and classification. Botanical nomenclature is exact and universal, but

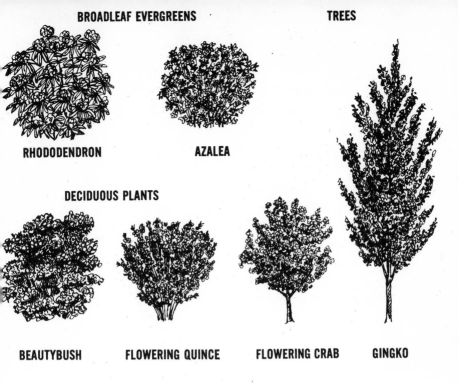

BROADLEAF EVERGREENS · **TREES**

RHODODENDRON   AZALEA

DECIDUOUS PLANTS

BEAUTYBUSH   FLOWERING QUINCE   FLOWERING CRAB   GINGKO

Broadleaf evergreens give bloom and exquisite style. Trees and shrubs of deciduous varieties offer infinite variations of form

it is quite unnecessary to understand this vocabulary to be a successful gardener.

Some plants are as generally known by their botanical names as by their so-called common names. For example, taxus is usually called by that name, although the common name, "yew," is sometimes used. When someone gives a plant a complicated name, ask for the common name.

The Names of Plant Groups (or types) are important to know when you are ready to ask about them or to purchase them at the garden center. Here are the key groups:

Annuals: Plants that live for one year or season. Most annuals are grown from seed. Examples: petunias, snapdragons, most vegetables.

Perennials: The term commonly refers to plants whose roots live year after year even though their leaves and stems die in the winter. Examples: day lily, peony, iris, delphinium. There are perennial vegetables, too, such as asparagus and rhubarb.

Evergreens: Woody plants that do not lose their leaves or needles in winter. White pine and hemlock are examples.

Broadleaf evergreens: Rhododendrons, holly, and some azaleas are in this class.

Deciduous plants: The opposite of evergreen. These trees and shrubs lose their leaves each winter.

Shrubs: Plants that have one or more woody stems and that do not grow tall enough to be called trees. They can be flowering or non-flowering, deciduous or evergreen.

Trees: Includes many small as well as large woody plants that are larger than shrubs. They range in size from the flowering dogwood to the stately oak.

Ground cover: Any low-growing plant, especially one that multiplies through spreading roots or stems that develop into new plants.

Some plants have both annual and perennial forms. Sometimes a plant which is described as an annual will actually live through a mild winter in your garden. Snapdragons occasionally surprise gardeners even in the North by coming through the winter. Geraniums in California are grown as perennials, while in cooler climates they are grown as annuals, and must be started again each spring.

Plants need air, light, water, and food. The plant takes in these elements through roots and foilage and manufactures them into new cells which produce growth, flowers, fruit and seed. To keep the manufacturing process going full blast, an adequate supply of these raw materials must be provided for by supplemental feedings by the gardener.

Before you buy any plants or sow any seed, give a little thought to what you believe will give you the most pleasure in a garden. Do you want the easiest garden to maintain? Choose the toughest sort of grass and pick out shrubs that don't need much pruning. Put perennials in the flower beds. If, on the other hand, you want your garden to provide lavish color almost all year around; if you want borders, rose gardens, and other elaborations, be prepared to finance the purchase of all the essentials and to give enough of your time.

Is the production of foilage, blooms, and food a gardener's only reward? Compared to boating, fishing, skiing, or golf, isn't gardening a dull, tedious chore? Let's look at some of its advantages. In place of exhausting competition, gardening offers the opportunity for contemplation, for reflection. It is an answer to the need for activity that has a visible end result. Gardening requires a regular expenditure of energy. To maintain a garden requires two to ten hours a week of labor. This work is not limited to a short season. It goes on for ten months in most areas. Through digging, bending, cultivating and carrying, the gardener continuously tones his entire muscular and vascular systems. Heart surgeons have recommended this exact kind of exercise to anyone looking for long, healthy life.

2

PLANNING AND LANDSCAPING

Each tree, flower, shrub or vine, each walk or path, each area of lawn, each building, plays its part in the effect you want—a lovely, comfortable, eye-pleasing place to live

Modern architecture demands a simple, harmonious landscape design, plants that will not overgrow in relation to the house size

The first and most basic thing you must do in landscape planning is to decide what you want. Do you have a small plot, where you want to plant just a lawn and some flowers? Or do you want to landscape a good-sized area, adding trees, vegetables and walks?

Survey your land. Walk around it, noting existing plants, walks, and other features. Pay attention to the view you see from various locations. You may wish to preserve or enhance an attractive view, and to screen a less desirable one. The shrubs, plants, trees, even the paving, all play their part.

The Lay of Your Land Is Important. Notice how it slopes, climbs, falls, or rolls its way from boundary to boundary. Never assume land is flat. Look for bumps and holes.

Now make a rough sketch of how your land looks at

Typical errors in landscape design are shown here: too many plants, complicated design, and plant materials that grew too big

present, putting down as many measurements as you feel will be helpful later on. Draw in the existing plants, paths, walks, terraces, driveway and buildings.

Plants Are the Principal Decoration in Landscaping. It is impossible to provide complete guidance for the selection of plants, because this choice is so much a matter of individual taste. But it is possible to give some general suggestions. Plants dwell together in harmony when they are carefully selected, well-spaced and arranged to complement each other. This does not mean that plants of different kinds and colors can not live side by side; variety adds to beauty. Arrangement of your plants, however, is the key to good landscaping.

Location is the most basic consideration in arranging plants. For instance, in planning a flower garden, are you

15

Grass at top, bottom; retaining dry wall between the two levels

Rock garden with flowering and decorative plants retains slope

Shrubs in masses on the slope will hold soil, prevent erosion

16

locating it in a spot where it will get the sunshine and water supply it needs? Will it be protected from strong winds? Will you have room to work on it? Similar considerations apply to all the other members of your landscape.

Flowers are planted primarily for their color effects. Trees and shrubs form the masses in the landscape, and they are the best means of marking boundaries or dividing your garden into areas.

Architectural Features add precision and interest to your design. These include everything from paved areas, such as walks and terraces, to sculpture, seats, trellises, and fountains.

Grading Your Land. One of the things you may want to do is change the slope or level of your land by taking away, adding to, or moving the earth on your property to give you a better basis for your garden. While making plans for changes in grade, you should keep in mind the intended use of the land. Obviously, you want flat areas for garden beds and terraces.

How Large Should a Flower Bed Be? Four feet broad is considered the minimum width for a bed containing perennial plants. In essence, the size of the bed should be proportionate to the size of the entire landscaping area. Don't let the flower bed occupy an amount of space equal to that of other areas. One or the other should dominate.

Keep your landscaping simple. Remember, while straight lines are easiest to maintain, gentle curves help break up the formality. The following pages illustrate graphically landscaping dos and don'ts. Study them carefully before you complete your plans.

SCREENING WITH TREES AND SHRUBS

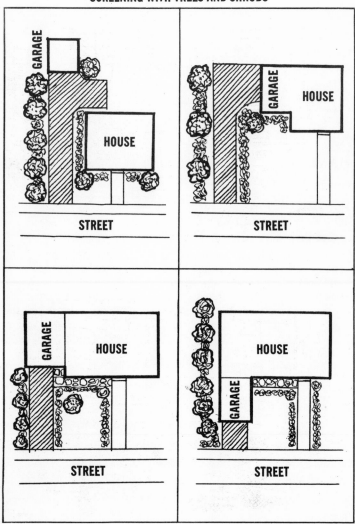

Bare views are uninteresting—soften sharp lines of driveways, walks and house with selective plantings of trees and shrubs

FOUNDATION PLANTING

Framing a window with shrubs— tall to the sides, short below *Corner: place larger shrub by window farther from the corner*

Between window and door, fill the space with tree-form shrub *At a corner, place large shrub diagonally out from the corner*

3

SOIL MANAGEMENT

**Readying the ground for
a lawn, for a flower garden,
for shrub- or tree-planting,
for raising vegetables—
whatever the soil management
problem, there's a solution**

Ideal garden loam (right) is mix of clay, sand, and humus. It can be built from poor soil too clayey (left) or sandy (center)

The Soil in Your Garden is much more than just a substance in which plants are anchored. It is a highly complex mixture of mineral particles, living organisms, and the residue of decayed and decaying plant material.

The basic idea behind soil management is to manipulate the soil you have into a workable, productive medium, suited to the growth of plants. Let's look at the major components of soil and at ways to improve their mixture for better plant growth.

Mineral Material comprises the bulk of the soil. Mineral material means rock, gravel, sand, silt, and clay particles, arranged here in order from the largest to the smallest kinds of particles. The difference in size between each adjacent pair is on the order of ten. A particle of sand is ten times the size of a particle of silt, one hundred times the size of a clay particle. No wonder clay soils differ so greatly from sandy soils!

Soil Organics include all the dead and decomposing remnants of previously living material in the soil. Under natural conditions, everything that grows eventually returns to the soil as a natural organic additive. In the cultivated garden, we must produce this artificially.

Organic material in a state of partial decomposition is called humus. Its beneficial effects last until it is completely decomposed. Humus holds moisture and soluble plant food elements in solution. It provides little reservoirs of water and food to which plant roots go for sustenance. When it is missing, we add it to soils overly endowed with either clay or sand.

There Are Three Classes of Soil – clay, sandy, and loam.

Clay Soil has the ability to hold water. This may be a help in time of drought, but under normal circumstances it has severe handicaps. It takes longer in the spring to dry out and become warm, and planting can be seriously delayed. If not regularly cultivated, it can become hard and resistant to the air and moisture that plants need to grow. How do you recognize clay-heavy soil? Take a handful, squeeze it, and relax your fingers. If it remains tightly packed, it has too much clay.

Sandy Soil. This soil is in many ways just the opposite of clay soil. It warms rapidly in the spring and is worked easily. It does not, however, retain moisture, and many of the foods needed for plant growth are lost. You can usually detect sandy soil by its dryness and looseness.

Loam Soil. This is the soil that is best for growing plants. Loam soil is a mixture of clay, sand, and humus. It is porous enough to let in air; it is sponge-like enough to hold moisture; it is workable.

If you find that your soil is in either the clay or sand class, good soil management can usually bring about a great improvement. Sand, humus, and even sifted coal ashes should be added to a clay-heavy soil until the mixture becomes workable. It will also help to leave clay soil roughly turned for the winter. Freezing and melting help break up the close texture.

How much humus and sand should you add to a clay-heavy soil? Our estimate is a bale of peat for a 10 by 20 foot garden bed. Spread sand over the entire surface of the bed to a depth of at least 2 inches for a very heavy clay soil, 1 inch for a slightly clay-heavy garden. Then work both materials into the top 10 inches.

If you find your soil is in the sand class, the solution is in liberal applications of humus. Without it, the large, loosely packed particles allow water to hurry through, carrying with it all sorts of nutrients in solution. This is called leaching. During hot weather, sandy soils must be irrigated and fertilized often. If you have a source of clay, add that to the sandy soil, and handle your peat as you did with clay-heavy soil, working them both in well.

You can buy humus or you can make your own. The latter is the inexpensive way. It also is the way that requires time, patience, and room. To make your own humus, you must have a compost pile. This is begun by spreading an 8 to 10 inch base of leaves and/or grass. On top of this, place kitchen wastes (everything, other than tin cans, cardboard boxes, bones, and glass jars). To this, add some store-purchased fertilizer and cover it all with an inch of garden soil. Wet thoroughly. Repeat this process regularly. Let the pile age through the winter. The following spring, the lower half will be ready for gardening use. The top half now becomes the lower half, and the process is repeated.

24

Humus should be applied to all gardens on a regular basis, not simply to correct a soil condition. Just dumping humus on top of the soil isn't enough. It should be spaded, forked, or tilled into the soil as deeply as possible, always at least 8 inches. Use it lavishly in the planting hole of any new plant added to the garden.

Animal manures are also excellent sources of humus, and even contribute to the nutrient content of the soil.

The Problem of Achieving a Proper Balance. As we have said, loam is the ideal soil as far as texture is concerned. Think of loam as that sweet-smelling, crumbly mixture of clay, silt, sand, and humus that gives most plants their best opportunity for good growth.

The exact proportions of these components is not too critical. If your soil has 10 per cent to 20 per cent humus, and the remainder is about evenly divided between the heavier particles of sand and the lighter particles of clay and silt, your soil will be a loam. A really good soil, mechanically speaking, is one that can be dug in with the bare hand, to at least a few inches of depth.

Plants Need Soil Drainage, which is to say they enjoy taking a drink from a water supply that passes by, but they react badly when they have to stand in wet ground for any length of time. The subsoil should carry away excess water. You can judge how well the subsoil is doing its job by observing whether water stays around in puddles long after a rain.

If your property is located on former farm land, your trouble may be "hard pan," a condition between the lower topsoil and upper subsoil caused by generations of plows, horses, and tractors, all of which carry part of the blame for compacting a plane of cement-like material. A hired tractor can drag a subsoil plow—a giant hook—through the "hard pan" and break it up to enable water to pass through.

Poor drainage caused by naturally low land is a more severe problem. Your trouble here is that the water table is so close to the surface your plant roots are always immersed. Drain tiles placed under the surface won't help. They would just fill with water and have no place to carry it to. The best solution is to grow plants adapted to wet conditions in any surface beds. Try wildflowers, such as trillium, jack-in-the-pulpit, and ferns. Wild shrubs for such conditions include blueberries, swamp azalea, and clethra. Inadequate drainage is also a cause of persistent moss. Roses, annuals, and other plants that require good drainage can be grown in raised beds or in large planter boxes and tubs.

All Plants Need Food. The basic plant food elements are nitrogen (N), phosphorous (P), and potassium (K). The easiest and best plant feeding program is the use of balanced commercial fertilizer according to the instructions of the manufacturer. You will find an analysis of contents printed on every bag or box of commercial fertilizer. It's required by law. A balanced plant food will contain nitrogen (N), phosphorous (P), and potassium (K) in the proportions of 1-2-1. Most fertilizers sold as balanced plant foods will be 5-10-5, or 6-12-6, or 4-8-4. Any of these will work well. Just keep in mind that 6-12-6 contains one and a half times the quantity of actual feeding elements as 4-8-4.

Acid or Alkaline? Some plants perform best in an acid soil, while some prefer a soil that is alkaline. Professionals use as a measuring stick a numerical acidity scale of 1 to 14.

26

The reading of any soil is known as its pH. A pH of 7 is perfectly neutral, neither acid nor alkaline. The numbers lower than 7 are acid, above 7, alkaline. Most garden plants prefer a soil that is slightly acid, a pH of about 6.5.

Individual specialty plants may require treatment of the soil to create a special environment. Rhododendrons and hollies, for example, need an acid soil. Snapdragons and asparagus need an alkaline soil.

To increase alkalinity, or raise the pH, add lime. To increase acidity, or lower the pH, add powdered sulphur. The addition of humus usually increases acidity slightly.

Just a word about lime. We are referring to ground limestone, which contains calcium. While not really a plant food, lime sweetens the soil (raises pH). It acts chemically on the potassium in the soil and increases its availability to plants. In addition, lime acts mechanically to give a better physical texture to the soil.

The pH can be measured with a simple chemical test. Inexpensive kits are available at any garden center. The home gardener mixes a small soil sample with a chemical solution in a test tube provided in the kit. The color of the resulting solution is compared with a color chart that gives an approximate pH value, close enough for home garden use.

The final important additive to any garden soil is a mulch. A mulch is any loose material added to the soil surface to inhibit weed growth, maintain an even soil temperature, and hold moisture in the soil during summer heat. Peat, buckwheat or cocoa bean hulls, pine needles, tree bark, or even newspapers can provide a mulch. We will speak more of the beneficial effects of mulch in a later chapter.

4

LAWN MAKING AND MAINTENANCE

A good lawn results from
a combination of proper soil,
proper preparation, proper
seeding, proper irrigation—
and large quantities of
fertilizer and elbow grease!

Lawn making: 1. Break soil; spread humus; till again. 2. Spread lawn food, lime, till. 3. Rake smooth with a hard-toothed rake

4. Spread seed evenly at recommended rate. 5. Rake gently with a spring-toothed rake. 6. Water softly, and continue to keep moist

30

Establishing a New Lawn doesn't have to be a back-breaking chore. First, make sure that you have the basic hand tools. (See check list, Chapter 10.) If you decide not to hire a tilling service, consider renting or buying a power garden tiller. And if your lawn is to be started from seed, use a lawn spreader—if possible, the kind which marks the edge of each path as you spread seed, chemicals, or lawn food. This useful device will pay for itself in seed and fertilizer savings.

Other necessary supplies include grass seed (or plugs, sprigs, or sod), humus, lawn food, and probably lime (ground limestone). The quantity of each can be determined by your garden center from your measurements of the area to be planted. Be sure to compute sun and shade areas separately, for they require different treatment.

Choosing the Right Grass for your garden will depend upon where you live, the amount of sun your lawn will receive, the amount of watering you are prepared to give it, and the use to which you will put the lawn area.

If you live in the North, you will want to consider some of the mixtures of grass seed containing several of the following grasses:

Kentucky bluegrass, of which many fine varieties, strains, and one patented new variety (Windsor) are available, is truly called the greatest of grasses. Its fine texture, deep, thick turf and magnificent color recommend it for your garden. Ask your nurseryman what the best mixture is for you. Ask, too, about weed seed content. It pays to buy the more expensive seed mixtures, which have a minimum of weed seed.

Poa trivialis, also a bluegrass, will substitute for Kentucky bluegrass in quality shady-lawn mixtures. All bluegrasses love rich, slightly acid or neutral soils and cool weather.

Creeping red fescue or Chewings fescue is fine-bladed, but somewhat more wiry than bluegrass and more tolerant of poor or sandy soil. It is good insurance to have some in a mix for northern areas.

Bent grass is sown or planted in plugs or sod as a luxury grass. It needs an immense amount of care. Its presence in a seed mixture means the addition of a fine-textured grass to the lawn.

Filler and "nurse" grasses are added to seed mixtures to bulk up the package and give a quick growth. They include redtop and rye grass. They are short-lived, and when they disappear the gardener is confronted with bare places where crab grass can easily start.

Meyer Zoysia can be grown in many regions of the North. The farther north it is grown, the longer it takes to get established. (See southern grasses below for more on Zoysias.) It is excellent in the summertime when turf matures; it solves crab grass problems. In the North this grass turns brown in winter.

White clover is not a grass, but is often sown for its solid green covering quality. It becomes slippery with traffic and can stain clothing.

In the South, lawns are started mostly from sprigs, plugs, and sod. These are the principal varieties:

Bermuda grass is thought by many to be the South's finest all-around grass. It will cover an entire area in practically any soil. In full sun or shade, Bermuda—which may be started from seed or from runner rootstocks, called "stolons"—grows into a dense turf. It is somewhat difficult to mow and tends to spread quickly to flower beds, so it does need some care.

Zoysia grass is among the best southern grasses. It will grow into an extremely dense turf that needs little mowing. Planted from plugs, Zoysia soon crowds out weeds.

St. Augustine (Charleston) grass is a coarse grass, but it grows in either full sun or shade in the lower and middle South. It is started from sprigs.

Centipede grass is a tough grass that does well in sandy soils. Although known as a grass that does not have to be mowed, it does need an occasional trim for a smooth look. Start it from either sprigs or seeds.

Carpet grass forms a beautiful turf, but prefers a moist soil. It grows best in lower and middle regions of the South.

Dichondra is not actually a grass, but a creeping plant with small, heart-shaped leaves. It is used quite successfully as grass substitute in California and the Southwest and needs only a couple of mowings per year.

Italian rye grass is used in the South as a winter grass to cover for winter-bashful permanent grasses. It does not inhibit their awakening the following spring.

Preparing the Soil is the major task in starting a new lawn. If you decide to do it yourself, by all means use a rotary garden tiller. You can rent one for ten to fifteen dollars a day, but it is a good tool to own outright if you plan to grow flowers and vegetables as well as grass. With it, you can easily till ¼ to ½ acre in one day. This admirable machine loosens and pulverizes the soil, and renders it ideal for seeding. It enables you to mix in humus, fertilizer, and lime, as you would stir ingredients into a cake batter.

If you decide not to rent or buy a tiller, you must turn the soil or old sod by hand. Try both a spading fork and a shovel to find out which works best in your soil. Proceed in successive lines across the lawn area, cutting out slices of sod 8 inches wide and 4 to 6 inches thick. Flip each one over and return it to its place upside down.

Don't worry about smallest rocks. Pick up fist-size and larger ones; throw them into a nearby wheelbarrow for later removal. Really big boulders can sometimes be pried out with the use of a stout log or 2 x 4. If they are at least 6 inches under the surface and not more than a foot or two wide, leave them where they are.

Having turned the soil over in clumps, you now have a very bumpy surface. Peat or other humus can be added at this point and incorporated into the upper soil mix by cultivation with a long-handled cultivating tool. Don't spare the humus; use half a bale for each 100 square feet, and more if the soil runs heavily to clay or sand. Just dump a half bale in the center of each 100-square-foot area and spread it with a cultivator or rake. Work this humus in evenly as you break the clumps of soil into smaller parts with the cultivator.

Peat can be spread by hand and with a rake before breaking the soil clumps, but it is difficult to spread lime and fertilizer when the surface is so uneven. Wait until the soil clumps and peat are combined into a fairly smooth topsoil, then add lime and fertilizer. Go back over the whole area again with your cultivator, working the lime and fertilizer into the mix to a depth of several inches. This further cultivation will make an even smoother surface—one that now contains humus, lime, and fertilizer.

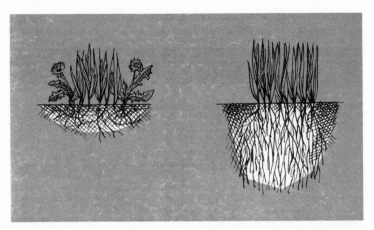

Daily light watering (left) grows shallow grass roots that die in summer drought. Weekly deep watering (right) creates strong roots

Both lime and fertilizer can be spread most easily by using a spreader. To figure accurately the quantity of lime to add, you must test your soil. The soil test kit will contain instructions on how much lime to add to raise the pH—a chemical term expressing degree of acidity or alkalinity—to a desirable level. Most grasses do best at a pH of between 6 and 7 (slightly acid). Remember, lime benefits the soil mechanically and helps release nutrient elements, so it can be added to any lawn with a pH of less than 7. If you do not test the soil, the use of 5 to 8 pounds per 100 square feet is safe.

Lawn fertilizer should be nitrogen-heavy, and preferably of the new slow-releasing type. The amount to use depends upon the exact formulation of the brand you purchase. Complete application rates will appear on the bag. Spread it over the soil, using the fertilizer spreader.

After spreading fertilizer and lime, you can go directly to seeding the lawn, or you may need one more cultivation if the surface still seems too rough—this time with a hard-toothed rake—to prepare the final seed bed. The soil should be finely granulated and smooth. Seed will lodge between the grains of soil and only a light raking with a spring-toothed rake will be necessary to cover them. Vigorous raking should be avoided, since seed should never have more than a very light covering—about 1/8 inch of soil.

Rolling the lawn is not necessary. A fine sprinkling of water will bring the seed into intimate contact with soil particles, and this is all that is necessary for germination. Keep the new lawn wet until it has safely germinated and is growing well.

Lawn Care and Maintenance. Once you have installed your lawn, you can see a great deal of money and effort go to waste if you do not give it regular care. The first and most important principle of lawn care is frequent and adequate feeding. Healthy grasses of the desirable types, such as bluegrasses and fescues, can thrive only with lots of food. When they grow abundantly, there is no room for weeds. You can prevent weeds by feeding, and at the same time maintain a full, healthy, and even turf that will carpet your garden with luxuriant beauty in all seasons. Fertilizer costs money, of course. But, if you have decided you want a good lawn, you can have it through feeding the grass plants. High-N lawn food, the kind that feeds over a period of time and safely, is a wise choice. A fertilizer with N of 20 need only be applied twice during the growing season. Winter color will be better because of it. Figure about 20 pounds of nitrogen per 1,000 square feet of lawn at each feeding. If you pass up our high-N advice and use a 9-6-3 food, be sure to water in each feeding directly after application.

For grass growing under trees, feed at least twice the recommended rate at each application. Many home gardeners complain they can't grow grass in the shade, when what they really mean is that they can't grow grass because their trees compete for the pitiful amount of plant food used. You can grow both grass and trees; the secret is plenty of food.

When to water and how much? Some gardeners water and some don't. Generally, watering is a good idea if you have had no rain for a week, and if you water deeply each time. Shallow watering, no matter how frequent, does not encourage deep root growth, and as a result the grass plants are in danger whenever you skip the irrigation. If you do water, use enough to soak the sod to a depth of several inches. Water only in the absence of rain, and then only once each week.

Automatic, underground sprinkler systems are the ultimate in convenience. If you want a really fine lawn, and can afford a few hundred dollars (less than two hundred for a small city lot), you can buy a fully automatic system that even turns itself on and off while you sleep!

How to mow the lawn. Mowing height is an important consideration. High mowing is preferred, to leave a maximum amount of leaf area for absorbing light and carbon dioxide. In addition, recent scientific research shows strong evidence that high mowing produces deeper root systems. If you think you want a 2-inch lawn, better mow it 2½ inches high. The finer varieties, such as bluegrass, can be mowed somewhat shorter, but tougher grasses should be at least 2 inches tall. Follow the practice of removing no more than 1/3 of the height at each mowing.

Crab grass and the birth of an industry. Whole chemical companies have sprung into being simply to satisfy the gardener's need for crab grass elimination. Their products work very well, if properly used. There are two ways to lick crab grass—pre-emergence control by use of a chemical that goes on before the crab grass sprouts (it is an annual), and a post-emergence chemical for use during the growing season of this ubiquitous weed.

If you had crab grass last year, you'll have it again this year unless you use a pre-emergence killer. Just be sure to get it on early, before April 1 in most regions. To be safe, do not use grass seed until at least six weeks after the use of the killer. Most pre-emergence killers are not selective; they kill all seedlings as fast as they sprout.

A post-emergence killer can be used any time after the seedlings sprout, and it will not injure lawn grasses. The earlier it is used, the better, since young plants are easier to kill.

Once the crab grass is killed, heavy feeding of desirable grasses will result in solid turf, and even the crab grass seeds that blow in from your recalcitrant neighbor's property will not be able to root and grow in the shade produced by your healthy turf. One final word about crab grass: Its seeds live in the soil for years, perhaps generations. So resist the temptation to tear up your old lawn if you can possibly build it up with food and seed. And introduce your neighbors to your own sterling practices, to cut down on the community supply of wind-borne seed.

Broadleaved weeds. These are really easy to kill and control. Just buy a weed killer labeled "for broadleaved weeds," apply according to instructions, and watch them wither. The principal broadleaved weeds are plantain and dandelion. Chickweed and other weeds can be eliminated with chemicals made specifically for them.

Rebuilding the Neglected Lawn. If it's a horror, full of weeds and bare spots, don't despair. Try rebuilding before tearing it up to start all over again. First, fertilize heavily—at least double the normal rate. That strengthens whatever good grass you have. Get pre- or post-emergence crab grass killer, depending upon the time of the year, and specific controls for the other weeds. Weeds will probably keep popping up all during the first season or two, but if you keep at them, you will eventually eliminate them all.

After the first blast of weed elimination, there will be bare spots. Treat these as new lawn areas. You probably won't have to cultivate as deeply as with a brand-new lawn, but at least loosen the top inch or two of soil in all bare spots. Lime and seed, as with a new lawn. After watering these patches, cover them with clear plastic sheets (paint stores now sell them as cheap drop-cloths), and you will not have to water very often. But make sure your seeded patches stay wet while germinating.

Even if the soil of your lawn area is really bad, you may not have to tear it up. You can simply add an inch of topsoil that is rich in peat moss, and seed right on top of that—after eliminating the weeds, of course. Your new seed will sprout,

DANDELION **PLANTAIN** **QUACK GRASS**

BUCKHORN **LOW MALLOW** **YARROW**

All of the garden and lawn weeds shown here can be eradicated with chemical controls readily available to the home gardener

and whatever remains of desirable grasses underneath will begin to poke through, too. You'll get a new lawn without running the risk of a crab grass infestation through too much cultivation.

The only other time "top-dressing" is really necessary is to bring a low spot up to level. Seed is not needed if only an inch or two of soil is added. The old plants will grow through.

Is Lawn Rolling Necessary? It has been found that new lawns actually suffer from heavy rolling. It compacts the soil, making it difficult for roots to penetrate. If you have a weak,

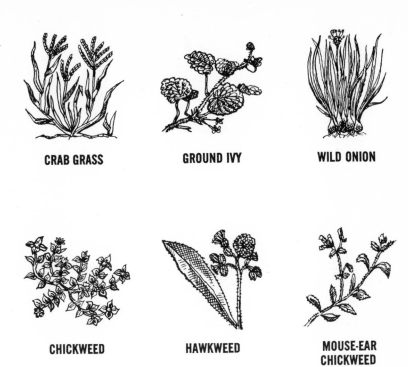

CRAB GRASS **GROUND IVY** **WILD ONION**

CHICKWEED **HAWKWEED** **MOUSE-EAR CHICKWEED**

Broad infestations can be eliminated with total coverage of area by chemical material. Spot control aims at the occasional weed

shallow turf that comes loose during the winter, it might be worth the risk of compaction to press it back, but even that is highly questionable.

Lawn Thatch should be prevented if possible, and removed when it is allowed to accumulate. Thatch is a soggy mass of decaying clippings and leaves that filter down among the grass plants. It was once thought that such organic material added a beneficial organic mulch. This material is now known to be quite harmful. Thatch is an ideal breeding ground for fungus diseases and harmful insects, and its value as a mulch is overshadowed by its many harmful effects.

Prevent thatch formation by using a grass catcher on the mower, or sweep the lawn with a grass sweeper after each mowing. The sweeper will really do a better job than the grass catcher, and is almost a necessity for autumn leaf removal.

Despite your best efforts at catching or sweeping, thatch will form over the years. Inspect for it frequently. When it does begin to build up, remove it before it becomes too much of a problem. You can do this by hand, with special rakes made for thatch removal, or you can do it—with a great deal less effort on your part, if your lawn area is of any size—with a gasoline-powered de-thatching machine.

Since this is not a machine for which you will have frequent need, renting one, rather than buying it, seems the wiser idea.

However you go about your de-thatching, you will be absolutely amazed at how much thatch you will remove from your lawn area—even if you feel that the lawn may not really need the de-thatching process. You'll find that you will take out as much as five or six bushels per 100 square feet—which will convince you that de-thatching is certainly worth the time and effort it takes.

Preparation for Winter. Don't let your lawn go into winter in need of mowing or with a covering of leaves. The grass should be mowed right through the growing season—as late as November 1, in some areas. Sweeping your lawn clear of all leaves will help insure its health for the following year. Besides, how much nicer it is to have a neat, well-trimmed lawn early in the spring. It gets the year off to a good start!

LAWN DISEASES AND REMEDIES

disease	grass	appearance	remedy
Brown patch, rhizoctonia disease	Bent grass, fescue, rye grass, Bermuda, bluegrass, centipede, Zoysia, carpet, St. Augustine	Round patches up to several feet in diameter during hot, humid weather, first wet and dark, later light brown or white; sometimes dark gray ring of wilted cobwebby grass at edges of diseased spots	Broad-spectrum fungicide applied when night temperature is above 70°
Dollar spot, small brown patch	Bent grass, Bermuda, Zoysia, St. Augustine, bluegrass, fescue, centipede	Small, circular dead spots 2" in diameter; may run together; cobwebby lighter area may show in dew	Use ample fertilizer; apply broad-spectrum fungicide fall and spring
Fungus—fairy ring, mushrooms, toadstools, puffballs	Bermuda, bent grass, bluegrass	Circles of bright green with inner portion thin or dead grass; fungus may appear after wet periods	Water, fertilize, aerate; apply Thimer, Tersan OM or Calocure monthly to area
Grease spot, spot blight, cottony blight	Fescue, bent grass, Bermuda, bluegrass	Circles several inches in diameter with dark, greasy borders; will turn reddish brown; disease is spread by mowing, running water; small, cottony spots common in South	Do not overwater; provide adequate drainage; use broad-spectrum fungicide
Leaf rust, stem rust, crown rust	Fescue, Bermuda, bent grass, bluegrass, St. Augustine	Small orange, red or black blister-like patches on leaves, stems; grasses may shrivel or die over winter	Fertilize and water for strong growth; apply broad-spectrum spray 2 or 3 times, 1 or 2 weeks apart
Leaf spot, melting-out, dying-out, going-out	St. Augustine, Zoysia, bluegrass, Bermuda carpet, bent grass, fescue	Leaf spots of various colors with reddish-purple edges; leaves turn yellow, then brown, die off; areas may die suddenly in hot weather	Beginning early spring, apply broad-spectrum fungicide at 1- to 2-week intervals
Mildew	Fescue, bluegrass, may occur in others	Powdery pale-gray patches in shady or poorly-drained areas; grass may turn yellow, shrivel, die	Sulphur, Acti-Dione RZ, Kromad or Mildex applied 1 to 3 times at 10-day intervals
Scald, snow mold, fusarium patch	Fescue, bluegrass, bent grass, Zoysia, Bermuda, carpet	At edge of melting snow, round spots with white, pink or dark fungus growth; may be dead patches several feet in diameter	Cut lawn in fall; apply broad-spectrum fungicide (not Acti-Dione RZ) first cold, damp spell. Do not fertilize in northern states after Sept. 15
Slime molds	All	Small blobs of white, gray or yellow slimy material which dry to powder	Wash down area with water after raking or brushing; if reappear, apply broad-spectrum fungicide

5

SHRUBS
AND
VINES

Shorter than the trees,
taller than the flowers and
vegetable plants, shrubs
and vines make an important
contribution to the
over-all plan of any garden

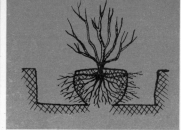

In moving a shrub or small tree first dig a circular trench around root area. Fork soil away and undercut root ball

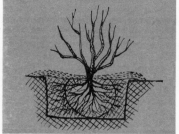

Tipping ball to one side, then the other, insert burlap under root ball. Lift shrub to new location. Replant at same depth

Shrubs and Vines add needed dimension to the landscape. Moderate in size, shrubs are bushy plants that help to fill in empty spaces and, along with the trees, which form high overhead cover, shrubs and vines are most useful.

Shrubs. Some shrubs are grown mostly for their bloom. Among these are Rose of Sharon (althea), lilac, and azalea. All, however, provide backgrounds, hedges, and screens of attractive and varying foliage. Few require any extensive modification of the soil. Their size varies from a few inches (heaths, heathers) to the giant viburnums and lilacs. Choose your first shrubs mostly for their architectural effect, and you will be surprised with their dividends in bloom, berries and fall color. Most good nurseries and garden centers have a wide selection, and the staff of such a place will be delighted to give you complete information.

Most shrubs have several woody stems. Some are evergreen, some deciduous. Blooming shrubs offer a wide range of colors, so wide that you can frame your house, screen an unsightly drying area, provide privacy for your outdoor "sitting room" or create a living fence in almost any color.

Color in shrubs. Orange-to-red flowering shrubs: azaleas come in a fascinating range of these shades; there are many roses in these colors; flowering quince makes a great show, and trumpet creeper can be grown as a bush. Yellow flowering: forsythia, golden currency, pea-tree, shrubby cinquefoil (this will flower for four months). Primrose rose and Father Hugo's rose make six-foot bushes, with eye-filling displays of flowers. Blue and purple flowering: althea, blue hydrangea, blue spirea, butterfly bush, smoke tree, lilacs of many kinds, chaste tree, Catawba rhododendron. Pink-to-rose flowering: flowering quince, beautybush, weigela, daphne, tamarix, pink snowball. White flowering shrubs: mock orange, star magnolia, many kinds of spirea (don't forget old-fashioned bridal wreath), white Rose of Sharon, white fringe tree—and, of course, white lilac, as beautiful as the purple.

Plant shrubs wisely and you'll have color all season long, greenery when the deciduous shrubs are not in bloom, and greenery the year around with evergreen shrubs.

Shrubs can be moved. Most shrubs will have come originally from a nursery. There they were transplanted during growth often enough to have caused their roots to branch into many tiny rootlets. Such a shrub can easily be transplanted into the home garden. Even after it has been growing there for a few years, the "good habits" grown into it in the nursery will still maintain the root spread within manageable

FLOWERING SHRUBS

plant	growing conditions	flower season	mature height	bloom color	best points
ALTHEA		7-10	3'-10'	Blue white red pink	Blooms all summer
BEAUTYBUSH		6	8'-15'	Pink	Massive bloom
BUTTERFLY BUSH		7-10	8'	White pink violet blue	Blooms all summer
CLETHRA	PS, A	8	5'	Pink	Fragrant bloom; black berries
COTTONEASTER	H	5	2'-7'	White	Bright red berries
FIRE THORN	PS, H	5-6	6'-12'	White	Fruit
FLOWERING QUINCE	H	5-6	5'-8'	White pink red	Spring bloom; informal hedge
FORSYTHIA	PS, H	5	8'	Yellow	Spring bloom
HEATH & HEATHER	A	1-10	6"-24"	White pink rose	Evergreen foliage
HONEYSUCKLE	H	4-6	6'-15'	White pink yellow	Fruit
HYDRANGEA	PS	7-10	3'-8'	Blue pink white	Summer bloom
LILAC	PS	5-6	6'-10'	White lilac	Spring bloom
MAHONIA	SH, H	5	3'	Yellow	Evergreen with blue berries
MOCK ORANGE		5-6	3'-10'	White	Fragrant bloom
MOUNTAIN LAUREL	PS, A, H	5-6	4'-8'	Pink & white	Flowers and Foliage
SPIREA	PS, H	4-7	1'-5'	White pink	Bloom
VIBURNUM	PS, H	5-7	4'-10'	White pink	Bloom often fragrant; fruit
WEIGELA		5-7	6'	White red	Bloom

Abbreviations **SH**—can grow in shade **PS**—can grow in partial shade **A**—needs acid soil **H**—good for hedges

bounds. As a rule of thumb you can lose about 30 per cent of a plant's roots and not seriously affect its health.

Evergreen shrubs are easy to move. Figure an earth ball about ⅔ as wide as the branch spread. Dig a trench with shovel, spade, or earth fork around the circumference of the intended ball and to a depth of at least ⅔ of the width of the ball. Having achieved this depth, you can reduce the size of the earth ball by forking soil away from the roots, leaving the roots intact at the edges of the ball. Work the fork under the ball until you can break the ball away cleanly. Now rock the plant to one side and wad a large square of burlap or other heavy material, accordion-like, under the tilted ball. Tilt the ball in the opposite direction and pull the burlap up around the opposite side.

Now comes the tricky part, particularly if the plant, with earth ball, is large and heavy. You must get it out of the hole. Secure the services of three or four friends or neighbors. Have each wrap a corner of burlap around a small stone. This forms a convenient handle. With the use of these handles you can now lift the plant from its location and carry it to its new home. Place it to the same depth in a new hole, tilt the ball to remove the burlap carrier. Fill the hole around the ball with soil about half the hole's depth. Then water liberally. After the water has soaked the ball thoroughly, fill the hole except for a saucer-shaped depression on top to catch rain water.

In any plant moving, compensatory pruning of the upper branches will help prevent shock, as will spraying before moving with an anti-transpirant such as Wilt-Pruf.

Vines. For coverage of banks, slopes, fences, walls, or to train on trellises, vines come into their own. Some, like the traditional ivy, grow rampant, although they can be limited with annual cutting. Some, like clematis and wisteria, have a flowering ability that is truly magnificent, rivaling the most prolific perennial or shrub. All can be trained, and with minimum care will reward the gardener with a lifetime of spectacular beauty. Consider honeysuckle for its perfume, Boston ivy, wisteria and clematis (for bloom), euonymous, pyracantha, climbing hydrangea, ivy, and trumpet vine (wonderful for attracting hummingbirds) for your first ventures into vines. Morning glories—an annual vine—will grace a fence or back porch with early-day blooms, and make a wonderful first growing project for children.

Some vines will grow up and cling to concrete, brick or stone without support; among these are Boston and English ivy, Chinese trumpet creeper, winter creeper, Virginia creeper. Other vines need a trellis, wires, or branches of other plants for support; among these are silver fleece-vine, trumpet honeysuckle, some wisterias.

Vines cling, with or without the support of trellises, in various ways. One of the familiar vines that clings by discs— short tendrils with small, sticky discs at their ends—is Boston ivy. A vine such as the climbing hydrangea sends out clumps of short root-like feelers called hold-fasts. The most familiar tendril-clinging vine is the grape—almost everyone has seen those springy tendrils wrapping themselves around any sort of support available. Twining vines cling and climb by wrapping their stems around either a support, such as a pole (honeysuckle, for example), or around another of its own stems (examples are wisteria, bittersweet.) If you expect any

FORSYTHIA
Mature Height 8'

HEATHER
Mature Height 6"-24"

Extreme example of the enormous variation in the size of mature shrubs. Consider mature size carefully before making selection

vine to climb a smooth surface, you must offer it support.

Vines are a sound garden investment. They will soften sharp lines, such as edges of buildings; they will give you foliage, often bloom—sometimes fruit, as well—at greater height than your cutting-garden plants; they will add beauty, when grown on trellises or fences, to the "walls" of your garden and screen for privacy as well.

Most vines are perennials. Once they are put in place they will make a cheerful showing year after year, with perhaps a little judicious pruning now and then to keep them shapely and away from other plants in the garden. There are a few annual vines as well, among them moonflower (blooms and sweet scent in the dark), gourds (for quick-growing shade and for the pretty fruit), scarlet-runner bean (for gay color), sweetpeas (for lovely bouquets).

6

THE FLOWER GARDEN

For beauty outdoors, and for bringing beauty indoors, you can have flowers in bloom—in all their infinite variety of kind and color— nine months of the year

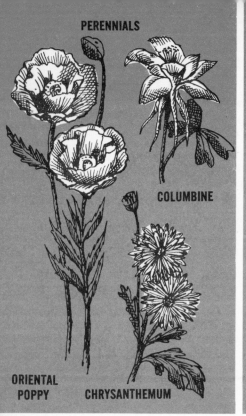

PERENNIALS

COLUMBINE

ORIENTAL POPPY

CHRYSANTHEMUM

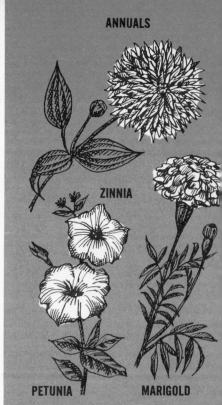

ANNUALS

ZINNIA

PETUNIA

MARIGOLD

With a little planning and an understanding of the needs of plants, anybody can have an abundant supply of flowers from early spring straight through autumn. The kinds of flowers you will be using in your flower garden are annuals, perennials, biennials, and bulbs.

Annuals Must Be Planted Yearly. They complete their life cycle—from seed to flower to seed again—in a single year or less. Thus, they die every winter, and must be started all over again each spring. The advantage of having annuals in your garden is that they are fast-growing plants, and will give you glorious color quickly.

How do you plant your annuals? You can start your annuals early by growing them from seed in your house or in a coldframe—a glass-covered frame that protects the young seedlings from cold weather. All you need is a container, soil, water, and a little plant food. Kits are offered which make this a simple process. However, most home gardeners who grow their own plants indoors for the first time tend to start them too early and end up with spindly, weak specimens when the time comes to set them out in the spring. Follow the directions on the seed packet. As a general rule, annual seeds should not be started indoors earlier than April 1.

If you don't want to be bothered with seed-starting, wait until planting time (April 15 to June 1, depending upon location), when the soil and air are warm. Then you can either plant directly with seeds, or else buy plants which the nursery or garden center has already started. These come in pots or in wooden trays called flats. The easiest container to manipulate is the peat pot because in the ground, it will disintegrate, mixing with the soil.

No matter which method of planting you use, the soil must first be prepared. If your soil is a heavy clay, add lots of peat moss to lighten it. If it is sandy, add peat moss to help it hold water. Pick a spot for your garden which gets plenty of sun (at least five hours a day). Fork and pulverize the soil to a depth of 8 inches, and water it.

If you are planting straight from the seed, sow the seeds and then cover them with not over ¼ inch of soil. Spread dry grass cuttings, burlap, or strips of folded newspapers over the planted rows. When the seedlings start breaking through, remove the covers.

If you are planting a started plant, simply remove it, earth and all, from the pot (except peat pot), dig a hole in the soil, and put it in. You must be careful not to harm the roots when you cut the earth between plants if you are using a flat. However, healthy plants will survive even the roughest treatment if the soil is prepared for them, and they are simply torn from the flat and immediately planted and watered. It is a good idea to give your started plants a little shade for a couple of days after planting. And be sure to keep the soil moist.

What care will your annuals need? After you have sown your annual seeds in the ground, the young seedlings will need thinning. The chart on annuals which accompanies this chapter states how far apart your flowers should be after thinning. Some annuals also benefit from "pinching." This means nipping off the terminal bud or the tip of the plant when two or three sets of leaves have developed along the main branch. This process allows the plants to become bushy and well branched; otherwise they tend to make spindly growth and produce scanty bloom. Some of the plants which will benefit from pinching are chrysanthemums, petunias, phlox, and zinnias.

Cultivation of the soil is important for the growth of annuals. Frequent, shallow cultivation is a good idea. Also, your annuals will benefit from the removal of fading flowers.

Generally speaking, if you give your annuals full sun, not too much plant food, and enough water to keep them moist, they will give you lovely flowers.

Which annuals should you start with? A list of the best annuals to start with—for ease of growing and maximum bloom—would include alyssum, marigolds, pansies, nasturtiums, Cosmos, Celosia, dwarf dahlias, zinnias of all types, the smaller snapdragons, Cleome, coleuses, impatiens (to grow in shade), asters, Nicotiana, portulaca, and petunias.

Perennials Form the Backbone of the Flower Garden. They are flowering plants which die into the ground each winter and send up new growth each spring. Perennials come up year after year, enlarge both in size and in number of plants in a given clump, and bloom more profusely with each season.

How do you plant perennials? You can plant perennials from seeds, from a division of the old clumps, or from nursery-bought plants. Dividing is simply the process of cutting the root mass of a plant into new plants. If the root mass is hard and woody (astilbe, for example), attack it with a sharp spade. Don't worry, you can be as rough as you like—use an axe if necessary. If the root mass is soft (iris, for example), cut it with a knife, spade, or simply snap it with your hands. Always look for the places where new growth will start and make sure one or more of those points appear on each new plant. Any year you feel like it, you can dig a perennial plant in early spring or late fall, divide it into several new plants, and plant each one as an individual. Just be sure to allow growing space for each new plant to reach its mature size. The growing space required for various perennials is shown in the accompanying chart.

To prepare the soil for receiving the new plants, spade the soil to loosen it up. Mix in peat, compost, or other soil conditioners, and add the plant food. Set your plants at the same depth at which they originally grew. Then pat down the soil and water liberally.

What care do your perennials need? For maintenance of your perennials, it is important to divide them after their third or fourth year, in order to prevent them from becoming overgrown. Certain perennials benefit from pinching, as well. To feed your plants, provide them with a complete plant food in spring, and again in midsummer. Watering depends on the particular plant: some perennials thrive in dry soil; others need periodic watering.

When winter comes along, it is a good idea to take certain precautions, so that your plants will grow back healthy and strong in the spring. After the frost kills the tops of your perennials, cut the stems and use them as a loose mulch. If the soil freezes deeply, add leaves, grass clippings, straw, or chopped hay. Mulch helps retain moisture in the soil for the winter.

Which perennials should you start with? The most rewarding for the least amount of care are astilbes, asters, chrysanthemums, Shasta daisies, dicentras (bleeding heart), hollyhocks, coral bells (heuchera), Hosta, day lilies, irises, lupine, peonies, phlox, salvia, sedum, and foxglove. If you are a beginning gardener, this list will give you plenty to do the first year or two. It will also reward you with blooms for the entire season from spring until frost, and provide interesting variations in plant form as well as possibilities for producing hundreds of new plants by dividing in future years. All of these plants can be purchased in the spring; some also in the fall.

Roses Deserve a Book of Their Own. If you really get interested in the "queen of flowers," you will want several good rose books. To get started in roses, just go out and buy a few

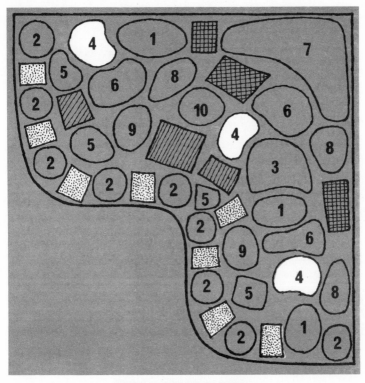

HOW THE GARDEN "GROWS"

CORNER GARDEN THAT COMBINES PERENNIALS (NUMBERED) WITH ANNUALS

ANNUALS:

▨ PETUNIAS
▧ SNAPDRAGONS
▨ COSMOS

PERENNIALS:

1. COLUMBINE (McKana Hybrid)
2. CORAL-BELLS (several varieties)
3. BLEEDING HEART (Bountiful)
4. ANCHUSA (Loddon Royalist)
5. ASTILBE (several varieties)
6. SHASTA DAISIES (several varieties)
7. DAY LILIES (six plants)
8. IRIS (tall bearded)
9. IRIS (Japanese)
10. PENSTEMON (Firebird)

sturdy plants, preferably Hybrid Teas, for your first venture. Plant them anywhere they will get full sun, in a well-drained soil. Add plenty of peat moss to the soil, water when the weather is dry, feed two or three times each season, and you will be a rose grower! Oh yes, there are a few bugs and diseases, but these have been overrated as reasons for not growing roses. All modern roses are grafted on wild stock, so plant the rose just so the union (a large swelling) of these two parts is at, or a bit below, ground level. Planting instructions are always provided by the dealer in case you forget.

For maximum growth and ease of care, roses should have a garden of their own. Figure an area of at least 3 feet by 2 feet for each plant. Thus, nine Hybrid Teas would be ample for a plot 6 feet by 6 feet.

Types other than Hybrid Teas have come into great prominence. Floribundas are fine for mass plantings and yield great quantities of bloom in vast clusters throughout the season. The growth is somewhat fuller than the Hybrid Tea, and a full range of rose colors is obtainable.

For height or for training to fence and walls, climbing roses may be selected.

Biennials Have a Two Year Life Cycle. They produce leaves during the first year and flowers during the second. After flowering, most biennials die. Though short-lived, they add much color interest to a garden. They are usually planted from seed.

Bulbs Produce Spring-blooming and Summer-blooming Flowers. Spring-blooming flowers from bulbs include tulips, daffodils, hyacinths and other smaller but equally charming flowers, such as crocuses. They may be planted in beds, along with other plants, or may be naturalized—planted at random —through the lawn or in woodland areas. Bed planting is best done with great quantities of bulbs, at least a few hundred per bed. In dealing with large quantities, it seems easier to excavate the entire bed to be planted rather than dig individual holes. Plant tulips, daffodils and hyacinths 6 inches deep and 6 inches apart. Smaller bulbs—like those of the crocus—should be set 3 inches deep and 3 inches apart. Shallow-planted bulbs rarely last more than one season—if they come up a second season they will be spindly and make a poor showing. Bulbs should always be planted in well-drained soil. Very little plant food is necessary, only a handful of bone meal in the spring. The fertilizer given to the neighboring perennials is usually sufficient. Caution—be sure to plant the bulbs right side up. The flat side is the down side!

Other spring-flowering bulbs which deserve a place in your garden are grape hyacinths (grape-like, purple clusters of bloom), and scilla and snowdrops, both of which come into bloom very early.

Summer-blooming bulbs, such as lilies, have undergone enormous improvement in recent years. Their range of color, size, and form is now so broad as to defy quick description. They will give a succession of bloom, if enough different types and varieties are chosen, through the summer and fall months. Gladioluses, too, have emerged in a splendid array of forms and colors. Each bulb produces only one flower spike, but that one is well worth the effort. Fanciers place them in rows in a vegetable-like garden. You may use them any way you wish, for color, for cutting, and for true garden beauty. Cannas, dahlias, and amaryllis will also produce

BULBS: DEPTH TO PLANT

INCHES	TULIP	CROCUS	HYACINTH	SNOW DROP	DAFFODIL	SCILLA	GRAPE HYACINTH
1							
2							
3							
4							
5							
6							
7							

showy bloom in the garden, and plenty of flowers to cut and bring into the house.

Some other summer-flowering bulbs you might like to experiment with are Peruvian daffodils (white or cream, several flowers to a stem), Mexican shellflowers (succession of bloom, fascinatingly marked flowers), caladiums (for their ornamental foliage), tuberoses (white, very fragrant), tritomas (tall red, gold, orange or cream spikes), all of which are planted in spring, dug again in the fall before cold kills the foliage, kept dry and cool, and planted again the following May. Tuberous begonias are spectacular flowers, and have an added advantage: they do best in partial shade and can be successfully grown in full shade.

Ground Covers Are Grown for Their Foliage, and their ability to lend interest to any piece of flat or sloping ground

PERENNIALS

plant	months of bloom	mature height	bloom colors	distance to plant apart	sun, shade, or light shade	special uses
Alyssum	5	12"	Yellow	8"	s	Rock garden
Anchusa	5-6	12"-30"	Purple, black	8"-24"	sh	
Asclepias	7-8	24"	Orange	6"	s	
Aster	9-11	18"-48"	White, pink, rose, purple	24"	s	
Astilbe	6	18"-36"	Red, white, pink	12"	s-ls	
Bellflower	6-10	8"-36"	White, blue	10"	s-ls	
Bleeding heart	5-6	12"-24"	White, pink	12"	s-ls-sh	
Candytuft	6	6"	White	12"	s-ls	Rock garden
Chrysanthemum	10-11	24"-48"	White, yellow, orange, bronze	12"-36"	s	
Coralbells	6	18"-24"	Pink, coral	6"	s-ls	Borders
Cyclamen	2-4 8-10	36"	Pink, red	6"	ls	Rock garden
Day lily	6-9	24"-48"	Yellow, orange, pink, bronze	24"-36"	s-ls	
Delphinium	7	36"-48"	White, violet	24"	s	
Foxglove	6-7	36"	White, pink, rose	8"	s-sh-ls	
Hosta	7-8	12"-30"	White, blue	6"-12"	s-sh-ls	Edging
Iris	5-6	24"-48"	White, blue, pink, yellow, purple, brown	24"-36"	s-ls	
Lupine	5	36"-48"	Blue, white, pink, red	10"	s-ls	
Monarda	7-8	24"-36"	Red	10"	s-ls	
Oriental poppy	5-6	24"-36"	Rose, pink, white, lavender, orange	12"	s	
Peony	5-6	24"-36"	White, pink, red	24"	s	
Phlox	5-10	24"-48"	White, red, lavender, blue	10"	s	All-season color
Pinks	6-10	5"-15"	White, pink, red	6"-12"	s	Borders, crevices
Primrose	5	6"-12"	White, yellow, blue, red	6"	ls	Rock garden, woodland
Rudbeckia	6-10	24"-36"	White, red, orange	15"	s	
Salvia	6-10	24"-36"	Red, purple	10"	s	
Sea pink	5-7	12"-15"	Pink	8"	s	Edging
Sedum	6-10	2"-24"	Pink, yellow, red	6"-12"	s-ls	Rock garden
Shasta daisy	6-10	24"-48"	White	12"	s	
Veronica	6-9	18"-24"	White, rose, pink, purple, lavender	6"	s	
Violets	5-10	6"	White, blue, purple	6"	s-ls	

where other plants are not desired. A few give additional dividends in their bloom and fragrance (lily-of-the-valley, for one). Many (pachysandra and myrtle, for example) will do well in either sun or shade. Some herbs (notably thyme) make excellent ground covers, particularly for smaller areas, such as planting areas in patios.

Probably the greatest modern advantage to ground cover is that it will virtually take care of itself. A few plants will spread to encompass any given area, and since all grow to a low maximum height, no cutting or mowing is needed.

Among the most widely used and recommended ground cover plants are pachysandra, lily-of-the-valley, ajuga (or bugleweed), Solomon's seal, trailing myrtle (periwinkle), ibiris (candytuft), and Hosta (funkia). Ivies also make good ground cover for either flat or sloping areas.

For larger areas, hypericum, honeysuckle, stephanandra, and euonymous acuta are recommended, along with trailing roses.

For interesting variation, varieties of artemisia (gray-silver), sage (purple) and sedum (white, pink, yellow) can be put to ground cover use, particularly in the smaller areas of the garden.

Flowers for Interior Decoration are a basic reason for any venture into gardening. With a little planning one can have flowers all year long in the South, and for as much as ten months of the year in even the coldest climates. The months in which you can expect certain perennials to bloom are mentioned in the accompanying chart on perennials.

How Should You Arrange the Plants in Your Flower Garden? Very little has been said here about the actual ar-

ANNUALS

plant	mature height	bloom colors	distance to plant apart	special uses
Ageratum	2″-8″	Blue	6″	Borders, rock gardens
Alyssum	2″-10″	Red, white, pink, lavender, violet	8″	Rock garden
Aster	12″-24″	Blue, pink, rose, white	10″-20″	
Baby's Breath	18″	White, red	12″	Good for arrangements
Calendula	15″-24″	Yellow, orange	6″-8″	
Candytuft	6″-15″	White, pink, red	4″-6″	Best in cool summers
Carnation	15″-18″	White, red, pink, salmon, yellow	6″-12″	Cool weather plant
Celosia	12″-36″	Yellow, orange, red, purple	6″-12″	Try the dwarfs
Cleome	48″	Pink, white	12″	Seed themselves reliably
Coleus	8″-12″	Red, green, pink	6″	Foliage color
Cornflower	24″-30″	Blue, red, white, pink	6″-12″	Great for cutting
Cosmos	36″-72″	Pink, white, yellow, orange	6″-18″	Stake tall varieties
Dahlia	18″-24″	White, pink, salmon, red, yellow	12″	Spectacular color
Forget-me-not	12″	White, blue	8″	Can winter over
Impatiens	6″-12″	Orange, pink, red	6″	Best annual for shade
Larkspur	18″-48″	White, salmon, blue, pink, red	12″	
Marigold	24″-28″	Near-white, yellow, orange	12″	Mass of color; very sturdy; easy to grow
Nasturtium	6″12″	Yellow, orange	6″	Some have edible leaves
Nicotiana	18″-24″	White, pink, wine	12″-18″	Very fragrant
Pansies	6″	All, brilliant	6″	Keep picked for maximum bloom
Petunia	8″-20″	Pink, white, red, blue, near-yellow	6″-12″	Grand bedding plant
Poppies	12″-18″	Yellow, pink, salmon, red	6″	Lacy foliage
Portulaca (moss rose)	6″	Pink, white, red, yellow	6″	Border
Snapdragon	12″-36″	White, pink, yellow, red	6″-12″	Stake tall ones; great color
Sweetpea	12″-24″	Pink, salmon, red, white	6″-12″	Try the dwarfs
Zinnia	24″-36″	Red, pink, white, yellow, green, bronze	12″-18″	Easy to grow; most colorful

rangement of plants within the flower garden. There is a reason for this: such advice means little unless the advisor knows exactly what plants the home gardener contemplates and the area of the country in which they are to be grown. Most plants will grow well, if differently, in any location. So jump in with a wide selection of things you think you would like to have in the garden.

Start with the perennials, singly if you wish to experiment, or in groups of three or more for more massive effect. Perennial garden beds or borders should be at least 10 feet wide and 10 feet long. However, large perennials of good form, such as peonies and irises, can be used in narrower beds along walks or driveways. Their foliage adds interest even when the plants are not in bloom.

The arrangement of a large perennial bed should be made according to eventual plant height, with larger plants to the rear. Don't worry about this at first—you can always transplant from one spot to another (early spring is best) and perfect the arrangement if it tends toward monotony. Be bold with colors. Nature doesn't fret when she mixes green, red, blue and violet—and neither should you, at least at first. After a couple of years you can always refine your color scheme, if you find that you have a few jarring notes.

It doesn't make too much difference in the beginning whether you buy one or several of a specific plant. Gardening is dynamic—every year's garden is different from the last. You can always add more of what you like best, and discard the things you like least.

After planting your perennials, fill in the open spaces with annuals, foliage plants and, for large uncovered areas, with

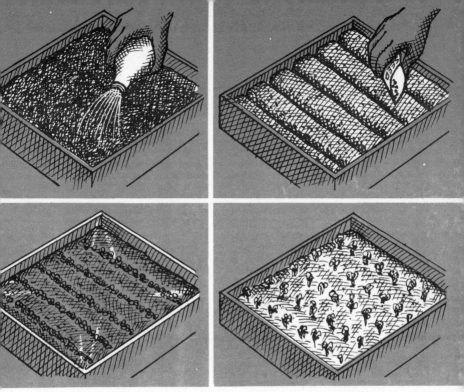

Starting seeds indoors: 1. Use a moist medium. 2. Place seeds in shallow furrows. 3. Cover and keep moist. 4. Thin or transplant

ground covers. Also, don't forget the color splash from spring-flowering bulbs. If all of this is against the background of some of the easier-grown shrubs mentioned earlier, you can't help but have a spectacular garden all season long.

After a few seasons of experience, the flower garden will prove you to be a real expert. Don't baby your plants—treat 'em rough, and discard the ones that displease you. Or, if you can't bear to throw a living plant away, give it to a neighbor whose plant taste may be entirely different from yours. That's the way to start a neighborhood beautification movement that will benefit the whole community!

7

VEGETABLES

Nothing bought at a store,
or even at a farm market,
can match in succulence,
color, eye- and taste-appeal
the lovingly-tended vegetables
raised in the home garden

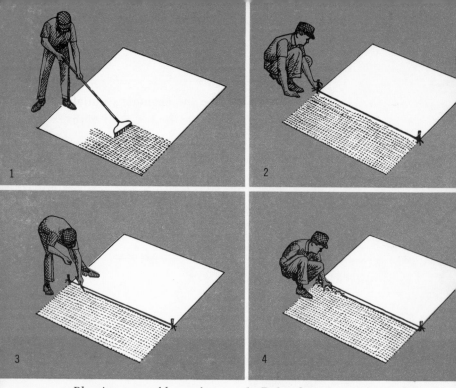

Planting vegetable seed rows: 1. Rake three-foot strip. 2. Lay string for row. 3. Dig furrow, plant. 4. Cover row, and repeat

Gardeners of All Ages enjoy the great hobby of vegetable gardening. As little as a 6 by 10 foot plot in the center of a city terrace can produce lettuce, green onions, carrots, radishes, and tomatoes for a hundred or more salads, all at a cost of less than two dollars!

The larger country garden can produce a year 'round supply of fresh, canned, and frozen delectables. A couple of hours each week spent in the garden is all that's required. Apart from the healthful exercise and the thrill of growing your own produce, home-grown vegetables are definitely superior to practically any you will purchase at the grocery.

70

Growing for Salads might well be the beginner's initial venture, and lettuce is the first crop to consider. Start with loose-head varieties. Although lettuce is usually grown in rows, along with other garden vegetables, it can be broadcast into a garden area in late winter for a very early crop. Successive plantings are made to give a continuous supply.

Radishes are another salad must. Children love to grow them because they can see results so soon. Many gardeners mix radish seed with a slower germinating seed, such as carrot, to mark the rows. The radishes are then pulled as they mature. Keep planting all season for a continuous supply.

Tomatoes come in many sizes, colors, and shapes. Start them from seed early in a window-sill flat, or buy seedling plants from your garden center at planting time. Give each plant plenty of elbowroom—about 3 feet each way. Your little started plants will look small and lonesome, but in July they will be 3 or 4 feet tall and literally covered with many pounds of ripening fruit.

Onion sets can be purchased by the pound and provide both tender, sweet green onions for salads, and mature vegetables, depending upon when you harvest them.

Vegetables for Cooking. Peas, green beans, spinach, corn, and many other favorite vegetables can be raised by the home gardener. Root crops, such as carrots, beets, and turnips, should be on your list. In addition to the "regulars," you will want to try some that are out of the ordinary, such as kohlrabi and Swiss chard.

Herbs, in addition to their value in flavoring both cooked and uncooked vegetables, will contribute exotic scents to your vegetable garden.

Preparing the Vegetable Garden. Just as in the case of the lawn, organic matter, lime, and fertilizer are essential to top production. Use as much peat or other organic material as possible. For fertilizer any good general plant food, such as 5-10-5, or 4-8-4, will do very well. Never use high-N lawn fertilizer, since this would simply produce a surfeit of foliage.

With these additives almost any soil will do well for the above-the-ground crops. Root crops, such as carrots, may not grow well if the soil is too heavy (clayey) or rocky.

Planning the Garden. The planting charts which accompany this chapter indicate how many plants you may expect to grow from a packet of seed. No attempt has been made to dictate a layout for your garden. That will depend upon how much space you have and the proportions of the area. Where we show a 20-foot row, this can be converted to two 10-foot rows or four 5-foot rows with equal success.

The rows of your garden should be long and straight, and the distance between rows should allow room for plant width, plus room for walking and harvesting. Minimum distances between rows are shown on the accompanying chart.

Would you like to skip the weed problem entirely? You can do this by using a mulch—any material that lies on top of the soil and keeps weeds from growing. It can be applied several inches thick and still admit essential air circulation. You can put the mulch down and plant through it if you are setting out started plants. However, if you are sowing seeds directly in the ground, you must allow them to grow to the intended mulch thickness before applying the mulch.

Be sure all plants in the vegetable garden get full sun.

This is essential. Consider the placement of any trees or buildings nearby, and plan accordingly. When putting in your plants, try to keep the taller ones from shading the shorties. Wide spaces between rows will minimize this problem. Rows laid out in the north-south direction will get maximum sunlight.

When Do You Plant? Ask your garden center or a knowledgeable neighbor for the earliest planting date in your area. It will seldom be before the end of March in the North. The cool weather crops can go in at that time—peas, spinach, and lettuce are examples. Later crops, beans, for example, go in about a month later. Spread out your plantings over three or four weeks. If you do this, a portion of your garden will mature each week and reward you with a fairly continuous supply of fresh vegetables.

Vegetable Garden Maintenance. Steel yourself to carry out a resolution to thin your plants. Particularly when you have sown seed directly in the ground, you will find your plants growing much too closely together. G   for full development by pulling and discarding unnecessary seedlings. The exact spacing depends upon the plant, and each seed packet will give you the figure.

Hand cultivation around the plants is a must, at least until they grow large enough to cast shade that inhibits weed growth. Even then, if you want a neat garden, you must hand-cultivate with a small scratching-type cultivator, and pull the weeds that are too near the plants. Between rows, where you walk, a mechanical cultivator—hand push or powered type—will save time and stooping. Here again, the gasoline-powered garden tiller really comes into its own. Mulching, as advocated earlier, will eliminate all of this fussy hand work if the mulch is thick enough.

Additional fertilizer should be applied at least once or twice during the growing season. Spraying, to keep down the insect population, is often essential. Of late, much consternation has been voiced concerning the safety of the practice. Prudence dictates following closely the instructions for the use of any chemical fertilizer on food crops. Read all labels with care. Be certain to stop spraying a while before harvest time; the exact safety period before harvest will be stated on the chemical label.

Watering—When and How Much? Observe the condition of your garden closely and continuously. There are many gardens that seem never to need irrigation, the rainfall in the area being quite adequate for most of the season. However, if your observation shows the soil to be dry to a depth of several inches, it is time to water.

However you apply the water—by surface irrigation through a hose that simply floods the surface, or by overhead sprinkling—be sure to soak the soil well each time. It should be thoroughly saturated to a depth of 3 or 4 inches.

Additional Delectables. Small fruits—strawberries, raspberries, and blueberries—are most rewarding. Ever-bearing strawberry plants will yield almost all season in small but steady quantities. Blueberries need an acid soil, and grow best in moist conditions. Raspberries are very easy to grow.

Some properties seem too small for much of a vegetable garden. Don't let space limitations discourage you from at least trying some kind of food plants. There's nothing quite like the thrill of saying, "Try this—we grew it ourselves!"

THE $3.65 GARDEN

CARROTS One 30' row. 120 plants, 3" apart		**25¢**
BRUSSELS SPROUTS Eight 30' rows. 120 plants, 24" apart		**25¢**
CABBAGE Eight 30' rows. 120 plants. 24" apart		**25¢**
CELERY Eight 30' rows. 360 plants, 8" apart		**25¢**
CORN Four 25' rows. 100 plants, 12" apart		**25¢**
GREEN PEAS One 20' row. 60 plants, 4" apart		**25¢**
BUSH SNAP BEANS One 25' row. 75 plants, 4" apart		**25¢**
BUSH LIMA BEANS One 15' row. 22 plants, 8" apart		**25¢**
BEETS One 25' row. 75 plants, 4" apart		**25¢**
BROCCOLI Three 20' rows. 90 plants, 18" apart		**25¢**
LOOSE HEAD LETTUCE Two rows. 50 plants, 12" apart		**25¢**
ONIONS Two 25' rows. 75 plants, 4" apart Plant sets which are bought by the pound		**65¢**
RADISHES One 20' row. 240 plants, 1" apart		**25¢**

8

TREES

Beauty and grace of form,
color in foliage and
in bloom, shade that cools
and shelters, a living
wall for privacy—trees
give your garden all these

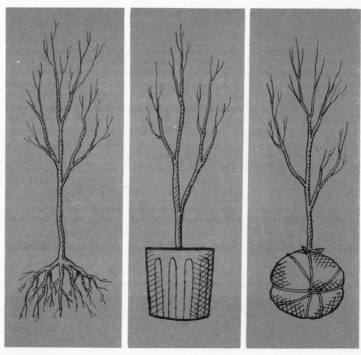

Bare-root stock (left) can be planted spring or fall. Container-grown or balled and burlaped plants can be planted at any time

What is your purpose in buying a tree? Is it for the shade, for the flowers and fruit it will bear, or just for the sheer beauty of the tree itself? Decide where you are going to plant the tree, and be sure to choose a tree whose size will be consistent with the size of your plot. And by all means choose a tree which you will find pleasing to look at. Your nurseryman knows which trees will grow well in your area. Heed his advice.

Nursery-grown Trees Are a Bargain. Their price is determined mainly by the size of the tree and its age; its rarity and speed of growth will also affect the price. The more time and effort a nurseryman must spend on a tree before he can sell it, the more expensive it will be. A slow-growing tree takes .longer to grow to marketable size than does a fast-growing one; hence, the nurseryman's investment in it is greater than in faster-growing species. He will charge more for it. A shrub-sized Japanese maple might cost fifty dollars, but if you were to grow it from seed, it would not reach its present size for twenty years. Unquestionably, the nurseryman can grow the tree better and in less time than the home owner can, and you pay for his investment of time at a bargain rate.

The giant maples and elms of the past are giving way to smaller trees. If your property is ½ acre or even less, it is well to consider the smaller trees exclusively. Within the range of trees available at good nurseries, specimens can be found to suit any lot size and plan. Discuss your garden plan with your nurseryman. He knows his trees and will be able to advise you when he sees your plan. Many nurserymen will be glad to take a trip to your home and base a recommendation on a firsthand visit.

Among the moderate sized, fast-growing shade trees of recent introduction, there is much to be said for the fine hybrid locusts now being offered. These include Moraine, Shademaster, and Sunburst. They do grow quite tall, but they are clean (no seed pods or thorns), healthy, and present a fine, lacy foliage that allows grass to grow underneath. They have been hailed as a possible successor to the elm. Sunburst has yellow-tipped leaves all season.

79

SHORT SHADE TREES FOR SMALL GARDEN AREAS

tree name	mature height	special needs	location	comments
Amur cork tree	50'		Average soil; sun	Withstands city conditions; black berries in fall; bark corky
Chinese chestnut	60'		Sandy loam soil	Two trees are needed for pollination; no chestnut blight
European hornbeam	50'		Moist soil; shade or sun	Often used for tall hedges, as withstands storms; strong wood
Goldenrain tree	30'		Average soil; sun	Withstands dry limy soils, drought
Horse chestnut	60'	Dense shade	Any soil; sun	Showy blooms; edible nuts
Japanese pagoda tree	60'		Any soil; sun	Pea-like flowers appear midsummer; withstands city conditions
River birch	60'	Check for suckers at base	Moist soil; sun	Usually has divided trunk; red, ragged bark
Russian olive	25'	Spiny	Any soil; sun	Silver-gray foliage; hardy; good as windbreak; withstands drought
Shadbush (serviceberry)	40'	Check for juniper rust	Moist soil	White flowers, April, May; red berries, June, July
Weeping willow	45'	Check sewer lines for root invasion	Moist soil; sun	Needs large water supply
Yellowwood	50'		Average soil; sun	White fragrant flowers, June; withstands drought

Another tree which is rapidly achieving very wide popularity, though not at all new, is the gingko, originally an oriental specimen. This tree is able to withstand adversities of soil, air, or climate. Its fan-shaped "leaves" (they are actually classified as needles, since the tree is a conifer) are quite unusual and turn golden yellow in the fall.

80

The golden sycamore (actually a maple) is extremely hardy, as well as colorful. Not even the salt winds near the seashore will affect it. Sunlight gives its foliage a yellow glow.

Red foliage will add a certain fascination to your garden. Few home gardeners would want a forest of red, but one to three red maples lend a focal point of color. Crimson King, a modern, patented variety of Norway maple, holds its red color throughout the summer, grows in beautiful, upright form, and takes little or no care.

The ever-popular dogwood blooms in white, pink, or red; and after the blooming season is over, the dogwood's fine foliage is a delight. Caution: It is safest to buy nursery-grown dogwoods and to shun "bargain" dogwoods that have been collected wild. Collected specimens are difficult to nurse through the first year. Once established, however, the dogwood grows easily.

A not-so-well known variety of dogwood is the kousa, or Chinese dogwood. It blooms after the native dogwood, well into June in most locations, and its huge blooms stay on the tree for almost a month.

Among the most spectacular of our hardy, disease-resistant trees is the beech. There are beech varieties that grow in columnar form (like the Lombardy poplar), or in regular vase-like configuration, or even in pendulant, weeping fashion. The colors of its foliage range from green through copper and purple to varieties that show three colors at the same time. The main stem is upright, strong, and covered with gray bark that is most pleasing during the winter. A beech planted now can live two- to three-hundred years.

Shade and foliage color are not the only reasons for

planting trees. Consider·the joy of having your own orchard of apples, pears, or peaches. An orchard may be as small as one dwarf fruit tree, or as large as your land will allow. If you use modern dwarf trees, you will never need a ladder to reach the fruit. And what is more amazing, fruit sometimes grows larger on the dwarfs than on the standard, normal-sized trees. The dwarf fruit tree is actually a "manufactured" tree, composed of two, or sometimes even three parts from different trees. The grafting systems used produce smaller trees but enable them to produce generous quantities of luscious fruit. One modern development is the "spur-type" fruit tree which produces fruit all along the branches, not just at the ends. In addition to fine tree form and fruit, these trees reward the home gardener with beautiful spring bloom.

Once the shade trees and fruiting varieties are chosen, perhaps you would like to choose some trees specifically for their color and form. Many unusual flowering trees are available which produce colors of gold, pink, white, and red in spring and early summer. Leaf form and wood color can also be considered to be qualities that lend interest and variety.

If your property is large enough, by all means consider the weeping willow. Many sophisticates shun the willow because it is so common. However, it remains one of our truly magnificent trees. It is easy to grow, quite healthy, ascends rapidly, and adds a dynamic aspect to the landscape with its softly rustling arms undulating in the slightest breeze. Be sure your property has a large enough water supply for its thirsty root system, and beware of placing it near a septic tank system! The willow's branches root easily and you can

82

TALL SHADE TREES

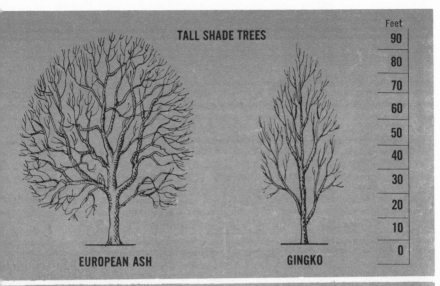

EUROPEAN ASH

GINGKO

Feet
90
80
70
60
50
40
30
20
10
0

SHORT SHADE TREES

HORSE CHESTNUT

EUROPEAN HORNBEAM

GREEN ASH

ORNAMENTAL TREES

FLOWERING CHERRY

FLOWERING DOGWOOD

FLOWERING CRAB APPLE

TALL SHADE TREES FOR LARGE GARDEN AREAS

tree name	mature height	special needs	location	comments
American sycamore	120'	Often sheds leaves in midsummer	Sun; tolerates poor soil, drought	Holds leaves all season
Black walnut	100'	Don't plant near vegetable garden; tomatoes react unfavorably to it	Well-drained, fertile soil	Nuts ripen October, November, but 3-5 years required on grafted trees
Box elder	70'	Weak; subject to elder bugs	Dry, sunny site	Good for windbreaks
European ash	90'	Plant male trees only	Any soil; sun	Come in slow growing and dwarf varieties
European beech	80'	Low-growing; plants will not grow underneath	Any soil; sun	Purple or copper leaf and columnar forms available
Gingko	80'	Plant male trees only	Any soil; sun	Pyramidal and columnar forms
Green ash	60'	Plant male trees only	Any soil; sun; tolerates drought, wind	Marshall ash is a seedless variety
Hackberry	80'	Difficult to transplant	Any soil; sun	Seed berries attract birds
Kentucky coffee tree	75'	Late leafing; pods of female trees messy	Any soil; sun; tolerates drought	Enormous compound leaves
Lombardy poplar	100'	May die during winter	Any soil; sun; tolerates wetness	Plant 5-6 feet apart for dense growth
Norway maple	90'	Requires shallow rooting	Any soil; sun	Good color all season
Red maple	100'	Requires shallow rooting	Any soil; sun	Leaves turn red-gold in fall
Red oak	60'		Any soil; full sun	Dark red coloring in fall
Shagbark hickory	100'	Difficult to transplant	Rich, moist soil; sun	Wind resistant, tough; tasty nuts
Silver maple	100'	Breaks easily in storms	Any soil; sun; tolerates drought	Good for shelter belts
Silver poplar	80'	Weak wood	Any soil; sun	Often develops suckers
Sugar maple	100'	Readily susceptible to diseases	Moist soil— acid or neutral; sun	Deep rooted; strongly branched
Sweet gum	80'		Any moist soils except heavily alkaline; sun	Lovely red-gold fall color; fruits last all winter
Tulip tree	100'	Wood breaks easily	Any soil; sun	June flowers, tulip-shaped
White ash	80'	Clutter from seed clusters	Any soil; sun	Leaves large, coarse
White oak	100'		Any soil; full sun	Red leaves in fall; bark whitish

use cuttings from the branches to plant more willow trees.

For smaller properties, the white birch, either a single specimen or in popular clump form, adds all-season beauty. The eventual height may reach as much as 35 feet, but since the birch is much taller than it is wide, space for it is seldom a problem. It will need a good supply of water.

For spring color, look into the golden chain tree, whose hanging spikes of golden yellow are a real eye-stopper. The fringe tree is appealing for its graceful, spidery white bloom. Flowering plums, cherries, peaches, and almonds all cheer the coming of spring with their colorful salutes. None of these gay performers is difficult to grow, and any one of them makes an ideal specimen of controllable size for lawn or border planting.

We have not spoken too much about the large conifer trees. Most of these are "forest" trees and do not belong in the average garden. We are referring primarily to pines, spruces and firs. The temptation for buying them is great because when they are young they are inexpensive and look "cute" in the front yard. But in a few short years they will tower over the house and dwarf the entire garden.

An exception is the hemlock. This is a forest tree, but it can be easily trimmed and shaped. It makes an ideal background for the garden when cut 10 to 12 feet high.

If you want an unusual accent, investigate the cut-leaf maple. Originally from Japan, these magnificent little trees are the utmost in refinement and style. A fifty-year-old specimen may be only 10 feet tall. The largest one we have seen is only 15 feet tall, and it is reputed to be over a hundred years old. These magnificent maples are not arti-

Tree planting: 1. Excavate twice root-ball size; mix humus, bone meal with soil. 2. Place tree to original growing depth; lower burlap

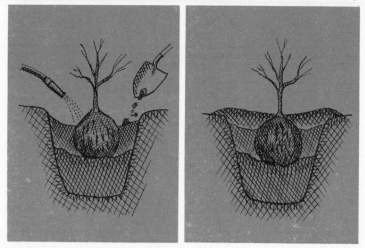

3. Fill soil around ball, tamping with foot until a few inches from top. Soak. 4. Complete fill, leaving saucer to catch later rains

fically grown in any way (not like the famous bonsai miniature trees), but their slow growth is a natural trait. If you do plant one, it could be considered as a shrub for its first fifteen or twenty years, and after that, as a small tree. They are available in both green and red-leaved varieties.

You can grow some of the newer patented varieties mentioned above side-by-side with a true living fossil. The Dawn redwood was known to scientists only through fossil remains until very recently when it was discovered growing in China. It has been propagated here since 1945 and has been found to grow exceptionally well in all regions. It is a fast-growing conifer with a pleasant pyramidal form, showing a soft green color in summer, and turning gold before shedding its leaves for the winter.

Planting a Tree is the simplest of garden operations. This is true whether you purchase your trees bare-root or with earth surrounding the roots in a burlaped ball or container. In any case, the most important thing is to dig a generous-sized hole, at least one-and-a-half times as large as the root mass or earth ball. Mix moist humus, compost, or well-rotted manure with the excavated earth. Do not use any powerful commercial fertilizer when planting. A cupful of bone meal may be mixed with the soil.

Replace enough of the soil-humus mix to bring the level of the hole up to the point that will insure the right planting depth when you place the root mass or earth ball on top of it. Try to build the under-table to a height that allows the tree, when finally planted, to be exactly as deep as it was in the nursery. Our experience shows that it is best to err on the high side. In other words, do not bury more of the tree's

ORNAMENTAL TREES FOR ALL-SEASON COLOR

tree name	mature height	bloom	fruit	autumn color	comments
American elm	90'			Yellow to russet	Tree experts hope for disease-resistant variety
Crape myrtle	20'	Pink			Southern favorite for all-summer bloom
European beech	90'			Bronze	Wide-spreading form; smooth gray bark
Flowering cherry	20'	Deep pink			Compelling spring display
Flowering crab	25'	White, pink, red			Few pest troubles
Flowering dogwood	40'	White, pink, red	Red	Scarlet	One of best small trees
Flowering peach	20'	White, pink, red			Grown for bloom; not too good a plant
Flowering plum	20'	White, pink	Purple		
Fringe tree	20'	White			Beautiful early bloom
Gingko	80'			Yellow	Extremely tolerant
Golden chain	25'	Yellow			Good lawn specimen
Japanese red maple	20'			Red	An aristocrat among small trees
Kousa dogwood	25'	White	Red	Scarlet	Blooms after flowering dogwood
London plane	75'		Seed ball		Tolerant street tree
Moraine locust	135'				Excellent, rapid-growing shade tree
Mountain ash	45'	White	Orange	Yellow	Large quantity of May bloom; fall berries
Red bud	35'	Pink, white		Yellow	Lovely spring flowers, winter silhouette
Red maple (Crimson King)	60'			Red	Deep red leaves all season
Saucer magnolia	25'	White, pink			Magnificent spring bloom
Washington hawthorn	30'	White	Red	Orange to scarlet	Fruit remains on tree all winter
Weeping willow	40'			Yellow	Pendulous, lacy branches
White birch	65'			Yellow	Striking white bark
White oak	80'		Acorns	Brownish-red	Sturdy; long-lived

trunk than was covered during its previous growth. Usually, bare-root stock will show a slightly different color below the soil line. Use this as your guide. In the case of container-grown or balled and burlaped stock, the soil line is evident.

If you are planting a balled and burlaped tree, set the ball into the hole with the burlap still intact. Release the burlap and fold it down into the bottom of the hole. It need not be removed, although if the ball is small and firm enough to enable you to lift the tree a few inches without its falling apart, you can take it out completely.

If your tree comes in a metal or fiber container, open the side of the container with tin snips, and then remove the tree. On very small trees it is sometimes possible to invert the can and tap the earth mass out. Do not do this unless you are sure the soil will remain firm around the roots. Then place the soil and root mass into the hole, using the same procedure that was described for the burlaped roots.

If you are planting a bare-root tree, spread the roots out in the hole so that they are wide apart and evenly spaced. Then add your soil-humus mix to insure that all roots are well encased.

After placing the tree in the hole, continue to fill it up with more soil-humus mix until it is 3 inches or so below soil level. Tamp the soil down thoroughly by walking on it to make sure the roots are in intimate contact with the soil particles. Then add a bucketful of water. After the water soaks in, continue filling until all that is left is a shallow depression at the surface to catch rain or subsequent water-ings. Keep the new planting well soaked for two weeks; longer, if you have planted late in the spring.

Stake Your Newly Planted Trees unless they are very small—about 2 feet or less. Several methods are shown in the accompanying diagram. Use as much staking as you feel is necessary. Staking keeps the newly planted tree upright and is most important during the first year's growth. Allowing the tree to whip back and forth in high winds can loosen its roots.

Protect Newly Transplanted Trees From Moisture Loss. This is accomplished in three ways. Pruning reduces the amount of leaf area and hence slows the transpiration of moisture by exposing less evaporating surface to the air. Wrapping the trunk keeps the bark from drying out. Spraying the foliage with an anti-transpirant, usually a plastic substance, inhibits transpiration and moisture loss. This plastic spray will not harm the plant in any way.

What Care Do Your Trees Need After Planting? Mulching the soil around the base of the newly planted tree will help to hold in the moisture that is so essential to its growth. Even so, water once every week or two throughout the first season of growth. Do not feed until the second season.

Soil scientists have discovered that the principal function of the tree's roots is to search for and transmit water to all parts of the plant. Experiments have shown that plants, even trees, can be fed through only a very small part of their root system. It therefore seems possible that the old time-consuming practice of boring holes down to a deep-root depth and filling them with fertilizer is totally unnecessary. Fertilizer applied on the surface is quite adequate. Feed the lawn under trees at least twice the recommended rate for the rest of the lawn.

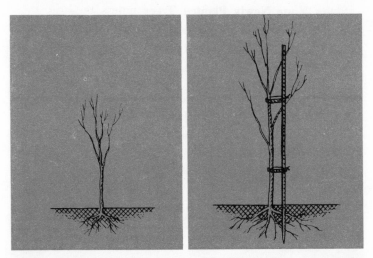

*Staking method varies with tree height. Newly planted tree under
3 feet requires none; a single stake anchors tree to 6 feet*

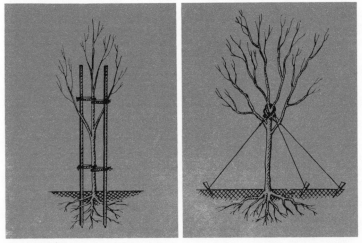

*Use double stake for larger tree, cables with hose protectors
for heavy tree. Always provide soft tie material to protect bark*

9

PRUNING

When you prune, you have a
twofold purpose—confining
the plant to proper size
and pleasing shape, and
keeping it in top condition
of health and strength

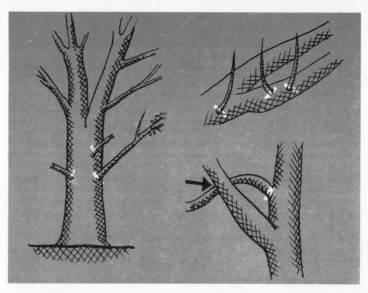

Plant health and appearance require the removal of weak or dead lower branches, sucker growth, and crossed or rubbing branches

Prune and Trim Your Garden Plants with a purpose. Harm can be caused by indiscriminate hacking, but much good can result from knowing how your plants will respond to your surgical practices. Generally, you trim a plant for a shape you wish to maintain. You prune either to remove unwanted wood or to get a growth response that will form the plant in the way you wish it to grow.

Trimming is practiced on small-leaved plants that are capable of giving a dense, smooth outer finish. If you do not trim a plant of boxwood or privet, its growth will be irregular and eventually tree-like. When such plants are used for hedges, we usually want the formal, smooth finish that only proper trimming can give. Once or twice during the growing season, these plants are manicured with an electric hedge trimmer or hand hedge shears. The correct trimming technique is to cut away only within the new growth that has appeared.

To keep a pine tree small and neat-looking is simply a matter of cutting the new growth in spring or early summer. The new growth appears as "candles" on each branch tip. Wait until these candles are several inches long, but catch them before they unfold their needles. Then cut off each candle at a point about halfway down its length. Where each candle is trimmed, several new tip shoots will develop. The following year, the outer finish of the tree will have an even more dense appearance. This illustrates one of the most important principles of plant response: when cut, a branch will usually form more than one new shoot.

Plants Respond to Pruning by forming new, multiple growth; denser foliage results when the pruning cut is made somewhere toward the outer tip of a branch. An easily observed example is "pinching back" chrysanthemum plants in spring to encourage the formulation of many flowering branches for the coming autumn. This is pruning that can be done with the fingers—just pick off the growing shoot of the mum when it is 3 or 4 inches tall. In a few days you will see that, below where you pinched it off, the stem has sent out several new branches. To produce bushy, compact plants for maximum fall display and number of blooms, follow this original pruning a few weeks later by doing the same thing to each of the new branches that has formed. They will also branch out. Three such treatments during the growing season will produce bushy plants covered with blooms in the fall. This process works on peonies and roses.

Most plants, including shrubs and trees, will respond

similarly to pruning when the home gardener wishes to get them to become more dense, to "bush out." Pruning, either to reduce size or to encourage dense growth, can be practiced with flowering shrubs. The trick is to prune at the time of year that will not interfere with the next blooming, and this depends upon whether the blooms come on old wood or new wood.

Surgery for Plant Health includes the removal of dead or dying branches in their entirety. Severed cleanly at the junction of the branch and the main trunk or larger branch from which it grows, the unwanted member will not regrow. The cut should be clean and larger wounds should be dressed with tree wound paint, which can be purchased at any good garden center. While the hand pruner can be used for smaller branches, lopping shears or saws are used for larger branches. Take care not to allow bark to peel back from the cut. For very high branches, a pole pruner or pole saw comes in handy.

After making any saw cut on a tree, trim the wound with a sharp knife to smooth it; use tree wound dressing.

Pruning Plants for Health also includes the removal of the unnecessary, enervating growth called suckers. Suckers are volunteer shoots that come from either branches or from underground plant portions. They are unsightly and sap the strength of the plant. Remove them in their entirety close to the trunk, branch, or underground portion from which they come. Some plants are grown on an understock of an entirely different material than the above-ground portion. Thus, roots used to support grafted lilacs can produce unwanted hedges around a lilac bush. Multiflora rose understock will occasionally grow a wild rose around your Hybrid Tea. As soon as these shoots form, take them off.

Not All Plants Need Pruning. Some can be injured by it. Certain plants are sold for flowering hedges but do not have the growth characteristics that enable the formation of a formal, dense hedge. Flowering quince is an example.

While herbaceous peonies are cut back beneath the soil surface each autumn, tree peonies should never be pruned. Rhododendrons need no regular pruning and grow dense and beautiful when conditions are right. However, to rescue an old rhododendron that has been moved to a more likely spot for better growth, but exhibits spindly, weak, widely separated foliage, prune it back. It will branch out again, although several years will be needed for it to achieve any size. Very large rhododendrons should have one or two trunks per year removed, instead of all of them at once.

Prune Early to Achieve Good Branch Structure in the case of fruit trees. A minimum number of well-spaced "scaffolding" branches are left on the young tree. When properly pruned during its first dormant season in your garden, the fruit tree will look very bare indeed. However, you have given it a fine start on a life of strong, graceful, healthy growth. The heavy structure which results from this early formative surgery will easily support branches and fruit.

Prune the Young Deciduous Tree just before or just after you have planted it. The object of this operation is to shape the tree for best future growth. Remove branches that are crowded, leaving just those that help the tree achieve a balanced form. This means that in future years all remaining branches will grow so as to allow adequate sunlight and air

97

PRUNING SHRUBS

shrub	garden value	pruning time	use of plant	comments
Abelia	Small, glossy foliage and late flowers	Late winter	Specimens, groups	Cut out older stems; if winter-injured, when extent of injury is evident.
Barberry	Ornamental fruits or foliage	Winter	Specimens, groups, in-formal hedges	Evergreen kinds need little pruning; hedges will not stand frequent shearing
Beauty-berry	Ornamental fruits	Late winter	Specimens, groups	Cut out older stems; if winter-injured
Bluebeard	Fall flowers	Late winter	Specimens, groups	May be cut to ground every year
Butterfly bush	Summer flowers	Late winter	Specimens	Cut stems to within a few inches of base of previous year's growth
Chaste tree	Summer flowers	Late winter	Specimens, groups	Cut stems to within a few inches of base of previous year's growth.
Clethra	Summer flowers	Winter	Specimens, groups	Handsome when not pruned, but may be pruned annually to restrict height
Crape myrtle	Fall flowers	Late winter	Specimens, in-formal hedges	May be hard pruned to restrict height; if winter-injured, when injury is evident
Flowering quince	Early spring flowers	After flowering, if necessary	Specimens, hedges, against walls	On walls tie in enough shoots for extension, cut back remainder to an inch of base of previous year's growth; hedges, shear after flowering
Forsythia	Very early flowers	After flowering	Specimens, screens, against walls	On walls tie in enough shoots for extension, cut back remainder to an inch of base of previous year's growth
Hydrangea	Summer or autumn flowers	Most of them in winter	Specimens	Bigleaf H., cut out flowering stems when flowers fade; Peegee H., shorten previous year's flowering stems in winter; Snowhill H., to ground in winter
Lilac	Spring favorite	Removal of old flowers important	Specimens, informal hedges	If some flowers are cut for indoor decoration little other pruning needed
Mock orange	Spring flowers	Winter, or after flowering	Specimens, in-formal hedges	Cut out older stems
Privet	Principally for hedges	Will stand frequent shearing	Hedges, screens	Amur P. hardiest; California P. liable to severe winter-injury in N. Y. area; Glossy P. hardy only south of D. C.
Rhododendron	Most ornamental of flowering evergreens	Removal of old flowers important	Specimens, groups	No regular pruning; if winter-injured, when extent of injury is evident
Althea	Summer flowers	Winter	Specimens	Shoots should not all be pruned to same height, lest plant look sheared
Spirea	Spring flowers, summer flowers	After flowering, in winter	Specimens, groups, in-formal hedges	Summer-flowering kinds, prune out old stems and shorten remainder about half, in winter

1. Pruning to shape a young tree, left, as received from nursery
2. Center: pruned upon planting Right: balanced growth results

circulation to reach all of the foliage areas for best health.

Look also for branches that cross or are growing in such directions that they will cross and rub in the future. From each pair of such branches, remove the less desirable one.

A Final Word About Pruning. Very little pruning is actually *necessary*. Plants can live without it, except for the removal of diseased parts. Since the principal purpose of most pruning is to improve appearance, it stands to reason that most pruning should be done only for the specific effects the home gardener wants. The gardener should begin carefully, experimenting with pruning in a manner which will not harm the plant, and observing the results. A few seasons' observation will teach the gardener the facts of plant growth and its response to pruning. This is the safest basis for a pruning program.

10

TOOLS

Having the right tool for
each gardening job is
half the battle; the other
half is learning to use it
so that you gain all the
help of which it is capable

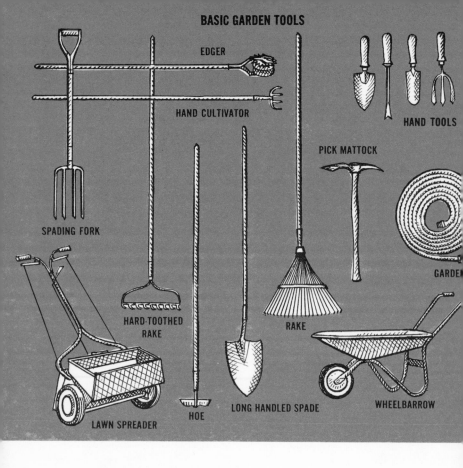

BASIC GARDEN TOOLS

EDGER

HAND CULTIVATOR

HAND TOOLS

PICK MATTOCK

SPADING FORK

GARDE

HARD-TOOTHED
RAKE

RAKE

LAWN SPREADER

HOE

LONG HANDLED SPADE

WHEELBARROW

Your Garden Tool Collection will start off small, but as your garden interests grow, so will your array of tools.

Every gardener has personal favorites among tool types. Some of our recommendations will be hotly contested by experienced gardeners, but since they are the result of our own usage over the years, we will stick by them.

Many tools are used in more than one operation, but here they will be mentioned only once.

Tools for Lawn Making. For what will probably be his very first garden operation, the home owner should purchase:

Shovel or spade for digging
Spading fork for turning heavy soil
Cultivator, long-handled, to break clumps
Hard-toothed rake, to pulverize soil
Spring-toothed rake, for final smoothing
Lawn spreader to distribute fertilizer, seed, lime
Wheelbarrow or garden cart for hauling
Pick mattock, for rocky soil
Garden hose, to sprinkle lawn
Sprinkler to distribute water
Hose reel for storage
Power tiller or tractor

Short or long-handled shovel or spade. We have always found the long-handled shovel to be the best of all digging tools. D-handled spades continue to be sold in great numbers, however, and we can only assume that their lighter weight and D-shaped top grip make them easier for use by women. We find the long-handled shovel to have far better leverage, wouldn't trade ours for a dozen D-handles.

Cultivators come in many lengths, sizes, and designs. The one we have found most useful for breaking large clumps of soil and breaking apart sod has five tines, each tipped by an arrow-like head. A somewhat smaller, plain-toothed cultivator is also quite useful. For lighter work, our favorite cultivator has a three-foot handle, and three flexible tines. A hoe can also be useful in lawn making.

Wheelbarrow or garden cart? The ages-old wheelbarrow is still preferred by most men, while women find the garden cart to be easier to handle. The advantage of the wheelbarrow is that it is easier to push in a forward direction, and in movement is more stable than the cart. Its disadvantage is that while moving it, the gardener must physically lift the weight of the barrow plus its contents.

Sprinkling equipment for lawn making includes garden hose of ample length to reach all seeded areas and a sprinkling head that will deliver a fine spray. The best all-around hose is the reinforced plastic type. Equipped with a newly developed easy-fastening coupling device, your hose can be detached for movement or storage in seconds. A hose reel is most convenient for storing the rolled-up hose, and makes the unpleasant task of coiling the hose unnecessary.

Powered lawn making equipment saves time and energy. If it is to be used exclusively for lawns, renting it will be more economical; if it is to be used additionally for large flower and vegetable gardens, buy your own. Ingenious multi-purpose machines have attachments for tilling, mowing, snow-throwing, and other operations.

A lawn-and-garden riding tractor is most worthwhile for large property. It can perform all the above operations and is also handy for many other jobs.

Lawn Care. Additional tools will be necessary for the maintenance of an established lawn. They include:

Lawn mower

Edger

Trimming shears

Lawn sweeper

Aerator

De-thatching rake

Weeding knife

Grass whip

The lawn mower is, without a doubt, the most important purchase you will make for your lawn. If your initial plans include a suburban lawn and garden riding tractor, your choice will be a mowing attachment for the machine. Otherwise, a hand mower should be the choice for anything smaller than 4,000 square feet. Unlike a power mower, you'll never have trouble starting it and you'll never run out of fuel. Take the hand mower to a professional sharpening service once each season.

For larger areas, the gasoline-powered mower seems to be a necessity. Your principal choice is whether to select a rotary or reel mower. The reel type, the basic blade design of which is almost identical to the hand-push mower, gives a superior finish, and is always self-propelled.

The rotary mower is the choice when you do not intend to have a smoothly finished lawn. Safety practices are most important in the use of a rotary mower. All manufacturers include safety instructions, and they should be followed to the letter.

Lawn grooming tools, such as the lawn sweeper, edger, trimming shears, and the grass whip for long blades or seed stalks, are important for that well-finished look. Although most gardeners handle weed removal with chemicals, a weeding knife can be used for the occasional upstart.

Lawn health is aided immeasurably by de-thatching (see Chapter 4) and aeration. Aeration involves putting holes in the lawn surface to admit air. Disc-type aerators as well as plugging equipment are available.

Flower Gardening Tools. Many of the basic tools already mentioned will be used in making and caring for the flower garden.   In addition, the following are necessary:

Hand trowel

Hand cultivator

Hand digging fork

Flower garden cultivator

Watering nozzles that soak rather than spray

Small hand tools are a necessity for flower garden operations. The trowel is used for digging and transplanting small plants from one bed to another, or from flats into the garden. The hand cultivator is most useful for close soil work around plants. The digging fork is useful for deep cultivation, stirring in quantities of humus around plants, and digging in heavy soils.

A brand-new tool, the flower garden cultivator, combines the advantages of the rotary cultivator and the scuffle hoe. It cuts weeds off under the surface of the soil, while at the same time stirring the top half inch or so into a crumbly consistency. It is convenient for working around and between plants.

Vegetable Gardening. Additional tools for vegetable gardening include:

Hoe

Wheel hoe

Chalk line

The hoe is used to break soil and cultivate it. Many vegetable gardeners prefer the scuffle hoe, since it is operated while walking backwards, and one need not walk over the portion of the garden just cultivated.

A chalk line can be improvised, with string and a couple of stakes, to lay out straight rows.

Shrub and Tree Care. For pruning and trimming add:

Tree saw

Anvil pruner

Pole pruner

Ladders

Hedge shears

Pruners and loppers have been described in Chapter 9. Our only bit of advice here is on ladders. In addition to a good stout painter's ladder, it is very convenient to have a very tall step ladder.

Pest Control Tools. The application of chemical sprays and dusts requires use of the following pieces of equipment:

Hand duster

Hand sprayer

Tank sprayer

Hose-end sprayer

Beginning gardeners will find dusting the easiest pest control practice, and are advised to buy a good duster. As the need is felt, add a hand sprayer or hose-end sprayer.

The Tool House. And, now that we have such a grand array of hand and power tools, plus the many items of equipment and supplies needed for the garden, what about a place to put them? That brings us to the tool house.

If any quantity of gardening is going to be done, a tool house of at least 10 feet by 10 feet is recommended. Hooks for hanging tools should be provided. Try to arrange to hang as much as possible on the walls of your tool house to leave the floor area for power tools and heavy supplies. Provide plenty of shelf space for chemicals, pots, and other small material. A potting bench is most useful.

11
PEST CONTROL

Bugs by the thousands,
diseases by the hundreds—
the list is frightening,
but the only trick to
control is attacking the
pests early and often

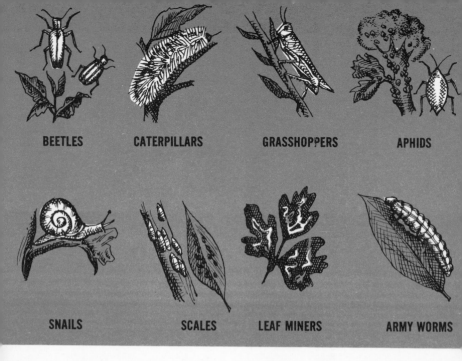

BEETLES   CATERPILLARS   GRASSHOPPERS   APHIDS

SNAILS   SCALES   LEAF MINERS   ARMY WORMS

Pest Control techniques begin with good garden practices. A clean garden—in which weed control is practiced through mulching and/or cultivation; in which debris is promptly removed—eliminates breeding grounds for pests and diseases, and makes the occasional pest easier to deal with.

Organic Gardening, while it may not be as efficacious as its devout adherents believe, will help create stronger, more resistant plants. In addition, the organic gardener is by nature a constant and tidy gardener, and his garden cleanliness will help to hold down the pest problem.

Biological Control of insects also helps. This is simply the encouragement of pests' natural living enemies.

Birds are insect consumers. By providing homes, food, and a congenial environment for birds, the gardener secures the services of hundreds or thousands of stout allies.

Chemical Pest Control remains the most effective technique available to most home gardeners in their battle with bugs and plant disease.

Spray or Dust? Dusting is simpler, since the dust is used as is—some formulations are packaged in their own applicators. One need only remove the top or punch a few holes in a duster-container to be ready to apply the contents. On the negative side, dust is wasted when used in a wind, and it tends to wash off as a result of rain.

Liquid control chemicals are mixed with water. Care should be taken to follow absolutely the manufacturer's instructions for both mixing and application. Harm can be done to plants by a too-strong application of some chemicals and, more important, the risk to the operator is increased. Care should be taken to spray or dust only in the direction of the wind. A mask that covers nose and mouth will also decrease risk.

Control Program Depends Upon the Plants You Grow. Normal landscape plants, including trees and shrubs, need little or no chemical treatment if their growth conditions are favorable. Look for specific insect or disease problems occasionally, and spray or dust to combat them.

Flowers and vegetables, fruit trees, and other ornamental plants will perform closer to expectations if a definite program of treatment is followed. The purpose is to prevent likely infestations before they start.

Generally, a good preventive program involves the use of what is known as an all-purpose or general insecticide. Most formulations of that description contain at least one specific chemical that kills chewing insects, one for sucking insects, as well as a fungicide to prevent fungus disease.

The preventive program begins in late winter or very early spring with the application of a dormant oil spray. Do not use this formula after growth begins. The plant should be completely dormant or injury may result.

For the remainder of the season, spray or dust once per week. In addition, spray after each rain, as much of the previous application will have been washed off. If it becomes necessary to water your garden plants, apply irrigation with a soaker-type nozzle directly to the soil surface.

When spraying or dusting plants, be sure to cover the entire plant with a finely distributed solution or dust cover. This means from top to bottom and on both sides of all foliage. It is not necessary to do more than wet the leaves with spray—keep the spray moving.

The Ability to Recognize Specific Pests will come with practice. While it is not our purpose to teach you to recognize all insects, it will be helpful to know a few of the most common insect pests that you are likely to encounter. Refer to the accompanying chart for more pests, and for control measures.

Specific control chemicals mentioned in the following descriptions are usually contained in general purpose insecticides. If you have recognized the infestation of one of the following insects, look for at least one of the applicable chemicals in the formulation you purchase.

Aphids. Mealy or wooly little flattish bugs that come in various colors. They suck the sap from plants and excrete a sweet substance loved by ants. This material forms a dandy place for fungus disease to live.

PESTS AND THEIR CONTROLS	Aldrin	Arsenates	Baits	Captan	Copper	Ferbam	Genite 923	Karathane	Kelthane	Maneb	Methoxychlor	Metaldehyde	Mitox	Nicotine	Ovex	PCNB	Pyrethrum	Rotenone	Sevin	TDE or DDD	Thiodan	Thiolate	Zineb
Aster wilt				●																			
Aphids, apple														●									
Aphids, other														●									
Bagworms											●							●					
Beetles											●												
Black spots, rose				●		●				●													●
Blight, general					●					●													●
Blight, chrysanthemum																							●
Blight, pansy				●																		●	
Blight, peony				●																			
Blight, pine tip						●																	
Blight, primrose				●																			
Blight, tulip						●																	
Botrytis																						●	●
Branch rot, Dianthus																							●
Bugs, sucking																			●				
Bulb flies	●																						
Caterpillars		●															●			●	●		
Clover mites																	●						
Curculios		●									●												
Cyclamen mites								●										●			●		
Damping off				●												●							
House flies			●								●												
Grubs	●																						
Leaf feeders		●									●							●	●				
Leaf spot				●						●													●
Mildew, downy										●													
Mildew, powdery								●															
Mites or red spiders							●		●			●	●		●								
Mosquitoes																					●		
Psyllas														●									
Rust						●																	●
Scale, hard & soft																			●				
Slugs, snails		●	●									●											
Webworms		●									●												
Weevils		●	●																				
White flies																					●	●	
Wireworms	●																						

Beetles. Don't try to be a beetle expert—there are 24,000 species! The adults bite and chew plants, and their young, while still in the larval stage (grubs under the soil), eat the roots of grass and other plants.

Borers. Different species of borers attack trees, shrubs, and perennial plants. If tree infestation is suspected, your best bet is to call in a tree specialist.

Iris borers are particularly troublesome pests. The best technique is to get them when they are in the leaves or roots at the time iris are dug and divided. Burn all leaves which show entry holes (brown) and inspect roots for tunneling borers. Cut these affected parts out and burn them.

Caterpillars. Caterpillars are the larvae of butterflies and moths. They voraciously attack foliage and fruit.

Leaf Miners. Actually, grubs that tunnel through leaves, these pests give themselves away through brown tracings visible on the leaves' surface.

Mites. Not really insects at all, but almost-microscopic spiders, the various species suck the juices of delphinium, strawberries, garden plants, lawns. Suspect them when plant shows a reddish webby appearance underleaf.

Nematodes. Enormous damage can be done in a short time by these worm-like creatures that infest roots, foliage, or stems. Remove and burn infected plants. Watch for withering, hanging foliage, poor bloom, root swellings.

Scale Insects. These tiny devils have an armored covering (hence the name, scale), stay put, and suck leaves.

Slugs and Snails. These devour leaves and flowers. Specific formulations are marketed for their control.

Thrips. They suck sap and leave silvery mottled foliage.

114

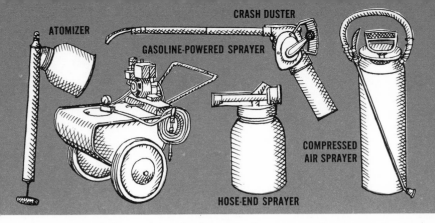

Sprayers and dusters give the home gardener control over weed and insect pests. Match the applicator to the chemical and job

DDT dusted on bulbs or corms is the best kind of control.

Plant Disease represents a much more difficult problem for the home gardener than insects. While it is relatively simple to see the actual insect at work, fungus, bacteria, and virus cause diseases whose symptoms are about as difficult for the layman to read as the symptoms of human disease. Consulting a "plant doctor" would be sound advice if he could be located. You might be fortunate enough to live near an agricultural experiment station, or perhaps trade with a nurseryman trained in plant disease diagnosis. Samples of affected plant parts can be sent to your state experiment station, but their condition upon arrival often prohibits accurate diagnosis.

The most common plant diseases are caused by fungus. Fortunately, the preventive spray program, using a general purpose spray, will take care of most of them, since such a formulation contains a fungicide. Specific examples of fungicides are Phaltan and Arasan.

Bacteria and virus-controlled diseases are just about impossible to treat. Remove and burn affected plants.

12

GARDENING QUESTIONS AND ANSWERS

Every gardener has questions he'd like answered about his gardening problems—here are the questions most frequently asked, and the authoritative answers

SOILS

Is black soil better than light soil?

The most important qualities of soil are texture, richness in plant food (N-P-K), and acidity. Texture can be tested by digging in and feeling the soil. Loose, crumbly soil is best. Richness can only be tested chemically. Be safe—add plenty of plant food. Acidity too should be tested. To lessen acidity add lime, to increase add peat moss. The blacker the soil, the more organic matter it usually contains.

My soil forms a hard crust and is hard to dig in. What should I do about it?

Add plenty of peat moss or compost, up to 2 inches or 3 inches spread on top. Worked in, this will greatly improve hard, compacted soil.

My soil is mostly sand. What should I do to it?

Your soil will need organic material (humus) to help it hold water and to give plant roots a purchase.

How can I prevent a bank (30 degree slope) from eroding?

Plant ivy, myrtle, or other groundcover. If flowering plants are wanted, try creeping phlox, sedum, ajuga. Or use steps or walls of stone, railroad ties, or other material.

I want to add a garden border where there is now grass. How do I make the garden bed?

Easiest way to do this: Rent a garden tiller. Otherwise, turn over the sod to a depth of six to eight inches. Break remaining surface with a cultivator, and rake out grass clumps, rocks, etc. Add peat, fertilizer, lime in process.

My property edges a swamp. How can I make the edges dry to grow perennials and vegetables?

Don't try. Your best bet is to go with nature and grow

plants that love boggy conditions. Try wildflowers such as trillium, Jack-in-the-pulpit, ferns. Wild shrubs for such conditions include blueberries, swamp azalea, clethra.

Why does moss grow on my soil? Is it too acid?

The principal reason for moss is abundant moisture. Correct drainage. Lack of fertility also encourages moss.

Should we plow or till our soil in the fall?

Actually, fall is the best time for soil preparation. Winter freezing and thawing improves soil structure.

Is there a simple test for soil acidity?

Kits are sold in garden centers for as little as $1.00.

PLANT GROWTH

How can I recognize nitrogen deficiency, and what can I do about it?

Plants appear sickly and small. Leaves yellow, hang from plant, and few new stalks or stems develop. Add a complete plant food (5-10-5 or 4-8-4) to supply other nutrients too.

My soil has plenty of nitrogen, but the leaves turn yellow. What should I do?

Your problem is probably iron deficiency. Chelated iron is available in small packages. Results will be spectacular if that really is the trouble.

Can fertilizer be applied as a liquid?

Yes. Several excellent brands of water-soluble plant foods are sold. Mixed with water and sprayed on plants, their nutrients are absorbed through leaves as well as roots.

Is there any way to obtain effects from plant food over a long period?

Yes, a recent development of the University of Wisconsin

indicates that plant food, enclosed in plastic with microscopic holes, will feed plants for more than five years without replacement. The university has obtained a patent.

How can I be sure plants won't die when I transplant them?

Important considerations are keeping root system intact within soil ball, preventing water loss through leaves by pre-spraying with anti-dessicant, and covering foliage with shade material during first few days of growth in their new position. Also keep well watered until established.

What is disbudding?

Pinching off flower buds while small to encourage larger flower from a single bud left on stem. Peonies, chrysanthemums, and roses are among plants on which this works well.

My tulips were planted four years ago. Now their blooms are weak and small. How can I improve them?

Dig and discard your bulbs. Plant new ones. This time plant deeper (up to 12″ deep) and they will last longer.

LAWNS AND LAWN CARE

What is the best time to sow grass seed?

Experts generally agree fall is best. Cool nights and abundant moisture provide ideal conditions.

Will sod or seed give the best lawn?

Either will yield a good lawn. Sod saves much work, costs more. Once established, sod or seeded lawn both require exactly the same maintenance.

Can grass seed be broadcast on an established lawn without any preparation?

You would waste most of your seed. Humus top-dressing should be thinly spread before such seeding.

I have killed all crab grass in my lawn. How can I make sure it will not reappear?

Maintain a dense turf through liberal fertilizer feeding, mow high, and inspect frequently for weak areas where airborne seeds might start new infestation.

Can broad-leaved weeds be removed by digging?

Yes, but complete extraction of all root parts is essential. Much easier to use chemical control, 2-4D.

Why do lawns continually need lime? Can I correct the soil acidity once and for all?

Decomposing roots and grass plants tend to make the soil acid, thus there is a continuous need for correction. Lime also has a beneficial mechanical effect on the soil.

What is the best way to edge the lawn next to a flower border?

All things considered, aluminum, steel or plastic edging 4 inches to 6 inches is best to prevent spread of roots.

What are the advantages, disadvantages of clover in lawn?

The best quality of clover is its ability to withstand drought. Principal disadvantage in the opinion of many is its appearance, which is different from grass.

FLOWERING PLANTS
Can I grow annuals and perennials in the same bed?

Yes, quite satisfactorily. Many gardeners use annual plants, purchased in growth at garden centers, to fill open places in the perennial bed.

How heavily should annuals be fertilized?

Feed annuals lightly unless soil is extremely poor.

Which annual seeds can I sow directly in the ground with the greatest chance of success?

Annual asters, cosmos, marigold, portulaca, zinnias, dwarf dahlias, nasturtiums, alyssum, celosia, calendulas, nicotiana, morning glories.

How can I best plan the locations of various perennials in the border?

Plant in groups of at least three of a kind. Alternate groups of different plants to provide all-season bloom over whole garden. Try to achieve a flowing pattern, pleasantly broken with plants of varying heights, texture of foliage, and color of bloom.

Should I plant closely to cover every bit of bare coil?

It is best, particularly at first, to allow plenty of room for plant growth and space to walk in and cultivate. Soil or mulch is not unattractive if cared for. Closely planted flowers are hard to take care of.

What is the best time of the year for transplanting and dividing perennials?

Fall is best. Very early spring is next. Transplanting during summer is risky, requires large earth ball. Exceptions: iris, oriental poppies, which should be divided in summer.

Should perennials be covered during the winter?

Greatly depends upon your area and the plants involved. Winter protection (evergreen boughs, hay, etc.) holds ground temperature more even, prevents thawing and freezing. Do not use leaves, which compact into a soggy mass.

How late in the year can I plant tulips?

While the ideal time is October, tulips can be planted well into winter; frozen ground ends planting.

Tulip leaves look messy after bloom. Can I cut them off?

You will deprive the tulip of needed sun if you do. One

solution is to interplant other plants to camouflage tulip foliage. Another is to bind foliage in neat packages with rubber bands. Remove seed pods to preserve bulb strength.

VEGETABLE GARDENING

When should soil be prepared for the vegetable garden?

As early in the spring as the soil can be worked. Three or four weeks before planting is desirable. First preparation should begin the previous fall for best results.

If I am to plant early crops, when do I prepare soil?

The previous fall is the best time.

Where should a vegetable garden be located?

The prime requirement is plenty of sun. The direction of the layout or of individual rows matters little.

What kind of soil is best for vegetables?

Any well-drained soil will do fine. If too clayey or sandy, add large quantities of organic matter.

Do different vegetable varieties require varying soil types?

Generally, all vegetables can be grown in one garden.

What is the best method of adding commercial fertilizer?

Initial application can be made just before planting and stirred into the soil with final preparation. Apply additional fertilizer during growth of plants as side dressing, cultivate into soil. Water after applying dry fertilizer.

Animal manure was once advised as an essential to vegetable gardening. Can I raise vegetables without it?

Yes. The principal advantage of manure, in addition to its fertilizing value, is the addition of organic material. This can be accomplished with peat, compost, or vermiculite. The home garden compost pile is an effective substitute.

What is "green manure?"

Crops, such as rye, grown for the purpose of adding to the humus content of the soil. They are mowed and the remaining plant with roots is plowed, tilled, or spaded under. When decomposed, this adds to the humus content.

Can vegetables be started early in the house or coldframe?

Those that transplant easily can—tomatoes, beets, lettuce, and some vine plants, including cucumber.

Should plants be thinned?

Yes, vegetable plants sowed directly into the garden as seeds will be too thick for best growth. Pull plants, leaving the spacing advised on seed packet.

Can vegetable plants be transplanted?

Yes, when very young, at thinning time.

How is the vegetable garden cultivated?

By hand hoeing, or power tilling. Mulching greatly reduces or eliminates the necessity for cultivation.

SAVING TIME, TEMPER, AND PLANTS

I am bewildered by the enormous number of problems in gardening. I want a garden, but hesitate for fear I'll have to devote all my spare time to controlling disease and pests. Would you advise me to forget about gardening?

Do not let potential trouble stand in the way of having a garden. Of the thousands of things that can go wrong, just remember that only one or two at a time are going to interfere with your garden success. To be a home gardener does not require you to become a walking encyclopedia of plant knowledge, nor do you need to know all the pests and controls. When you have a problem, attack it by getting

124

help from a knowledgeable nurseryman, county agent, or neighbor. Garden magazines conduct reader columns through which such questions are answered. Your library will have many books on specific garden problems.

What are the minimum insect control chemicals I should plan to use?

Purchase a general garden insecticide, and plan to apply every week to ten days as a preventive program. This will head off a majority of insect problems. During the season, obtain specific control measures for problems that arise.

My recently purchased home has mature apple and plum trees. Will I need to spray to insure insect-free fruit?

Yes, several times during the season. For easiest and quickest application, obtain a motorized tank sprayer of at least ten gallon capacity.

Are large, riding mowers worth the money?

Definitely, for any property of one-half acre or more. A 58 inch, three-reel riding mower will cut a half acre in about half an hour. Figuring twenty mowings per season, such a machine will save at least forty hours of work, and will pay for itself, compared with the cost of hiring labor to do the mowing, in from two to four seasons.

What is the advantage of constant maintenance of a garden?

A few minutes spent inspecting, edging, cultivating, and pulling immature weeds once or twice per week eventually "trains" the garden as well as the gardener. There will be fewer weed seeds to germinate, and wanted plants will grow better and fight their own battles with this kind of encouragement. Allowed to grow strong, a weed develops a root structure that almost defies extraction.

125

INDEX

A

Aerator, pp 104, 105
Ajuga, pp 64, 118
Althea, p 47
Alyssum, p 56
Annuals, pp 10, 26, 54,
    55, 56, 122
Anvil pruner, p 107
Aphids, p 112
Asparagus, pp 10, 27
Asters, pp 57, 58
Azaleas, pp 10, 46, 47

B

Beans, pp 73, 75
Beautybush, p 47
Beech, p 81
Beetles, p 114
Beets, pp 71, 75
Biennials, pp 54, 60
Borers, p 114
Bridal wreath, p 47
Broadleaved weeds, p 39
Bulbs, pp 54, 61-62,
    67

C

Cabbage, p 75
Caladiums, p 62
Cannas, p 61
Carrots, pp 70, 71, 72,
    75
Caterpillars, p 114
Celery, p 75
Chalk line, p 106
Chaste tree, p 47
Chinese trumpet
    creeper, p 50
Chrysanthemum, pp 56,
    58, 95, 120
Clay soil, pp 22, 23,
    24, 55, 123
Clematis, p 50
Clethra, pp 26, 119

Clover, p 121
Compost pile, pp 24, 57,
    87, 118, 123
Corn, pp 71, 75
Cosmos, p 57
Crab grass, pp 38, 40,
    121
Crocus, p 61
Cultivator, pp 103, 118

D

Daffodils, p 60
Dahlias, p 61
Dawn redwood, p 87
Day lilies, p 58
Deciduous plants, p 10
Deciduous trees, p 97
Delphinium, p 10
De-thatching rake,
    pp 104, 105
Dividing, p 57
Dogwood, p 81
Dwarf trees, p 82

E

Edger, pp 104, 105
Elms, p 79
English ivy, p 50
Euonymous, pp 50, 64
Evergreen shrubs,
    pp 47, 49

F

Father Hugo's rose
    p 47
Fertilizer, pp 24, 31, 35,
    36, 39, 61, 72, 74,
    118, 121, 123
Firs, p 85
Floribundas, p 60
Flower planting,
    pp 54-67
Flowering cherries, p 85
Flowering dogwood,
    p 81

Flowering peaches, p 85
Flowering plums, p 85
Flowering quince,
   pp 47, 97
Forsythia, p 47
Foxglove, p 58
Fringe tree, p 85

G

Garden cart, p 103
Garden hose, p 103
Garden tiller, pp 31, 73,
   118
Geraniums, p 10
Giant maple, p 79
Gingko, p 80
Gladiolus, p 61
Golden chain tree, p 85
Grape hyacinths, p 61
Grape vines, p 50
Grasses, pp 31, 32, 33
Grass whip, pp 104, 105
Green beans, p 71
"Green" manure, p 124
Green onions, pp 70, 71

H

Hand cultivator, p 106
Hand digging fork,
   p 106
Hand duster, p 107
Hand hedge shears, p 94
Hand pruner, p 96
Hand sprayer, p 107
Hand trowel, p 106
"Hard pan", pp 25, 26
Hard-toothed rake,
   p 103
Heathers, p 46
Hedge shears, p 107
Hemlock, p 85
Herbaceous peonies,
   p 97
Herbs, pp 64, 71
Hoe, p 106

Holly, pp 10, 27
Hollyhocks, p 58
Honeysuckle, pp 50, 64
Hose-end sprayer, p 107
Hosta, pp 58, 64
Humus, pp 23, 24, 25,
   34, 87, 118, 120
Hyacinth, p 60
Hybrid Tea, pp 60, 97
Hypericum, p 64

I

Impatiens, p 57
Irrigation, pp 24, 74
Iris, pp 10, 17, 58, 66
Iris borers, p 114
Ivy, pp 50, 64, 118

J

Jack-in-the-pulpit,
   pp 26, 119
Japanese maple, p 85

K

Kousa, p 81

L

Ladders, p 107
Landscaping principles,
   pp 14, 15, 17
Lawn food, p 36
Lawn mowers, pp 104,
   105
Lawn rolling, pp 36, 40
Lawn spreader, pp 35,
   103
Lawn sweeper, pp 104,
   105
Leaching, p 24
Leaf miners, p 114
Lettuce, pp 70, 71, 73
Lilacs, pp 46, 47, 96
Lilies, pp 10, 61, 64
Lime, pp 35, 36, 72,
   118, 121

Loam, p 23
Lombardy poplar, p 81
Loppers, p 107
Lopping shears, p 96

M

Manure, pp 25, 87
Maple, pp 8, 79
Marigold, p 56
Mechanical cultivator,
   p 73
Mexican shellflowers,
   p 62
Mites, p 114
Mock orange, p 47
Mulch, pp 27, 58,
   72, 73, 74, 90, 124
Myrtle, pp 64, 118

N

Nasturtium, p 56
Nematodes, p 114
Nicotiana, p 57
Norway maple, p 81

O

Oak, p 10
Onions, p 75
Organic matter, pp 72,
   123

P

Pachysandra, p 64
Pansies, p 56
Peas, pp 71, 73, 75
Peat, pp 24, 27, 34, 57,
   60, 118, 123
Pea-tree, p 47
Peonies, pp 10, 58,
   66, 120
Perennials, pp 10, 11,
   57, 58, 66, 122
Periwinkle, p 64
Pest control, pp 110-
   112, 125

127

Pests, pp 112-114
Petunias, pp 10, 56, 57
pH, pp 27, 35
Phlox, pp 56, 58, 118
Pick mattock, p 103
Pine needles, p 27
Pink snowball, p 47
Pines, pp 85, 95
Plant food, pp 26, 56, 72, 118, 119
Planting trees, pp 87, 89
Poa trivialis, p 31
Pole pruner, pp 96, 107
Pole saw, p 96
Portulaca, p 57
Post-emergence killers, p 38
Power tiller, p 103
Power tractor, p 103
Pre-emergence killers, pp 38, 39
Primrose rose, p 47
Pruners, 107
Pruning, pp 90, 94-97, 99
Pyracantha, p 50

R

Radishes, pp 70, 71, 75
Raspberries, p 74
Red maple, p 81
Rhododendrons, pp 10, 27, 97
Rose of Sharon, pp 46, 47
Roses, pp 26, 47, 58, 60, 95
Rotary cultivator, p 106
Rotary garden tiller, p 33

S

Sage, p 64

Salvia, p 58
Sandy soil, pp 22, 23, 55, 123
Saws, p 96
Scale insects, p 114
Scarlet-runner bean, p 51
Scilla, p 61
Scuffle hoe, p 106
Sedum, pp 58, 64, 118
Seed, pp 31, 55, 120
Shademaster, p 79
Shasta daisy, p 58
Shovel, pp 34, 103
Soil organics, p 22
Solomon's seal, p 64
Smoke tree, p 47
Snowdrops, p 61
Spade, p 57
Spading fork, pp 34, 103
Spinach, pp 71, 73
Spired, p 47
Spring-toothed rake, p 103
Sprinklers, pp 37, 74, 103, 104
Spruces, p 85
Staking, p 90
Star magnolia, p 47
Stephanandra, p 64
St. Augustine (Charleston) grass, p 33
Subsoil, pp 25, 26
Suckers, p 96
Swamp azalea, pp 26, 119
Sweetpea, p 51
Swiss chard, p 71

T

Tamarix, p 47
Tank sprayer, p 107
Taxus, p 9
Thrips, p 114
Tilling service, p 31

Tomatoes, pp 70, 71
Tool storage, p 107
Transplanting, pp 90, 120, 122, 124
Tree saw, p 107
Trillium, pp 26, 119
Trimming, p 94
Trimming shears, pp 104, 105
Tritomas, p 62
Trumpet honeysuckle, p 50
Trumpet vine, p 50
Tuberose, p 62
Tuberous begonias, p 62
Tulips, p 122
Turnips, p 71

V

Vermiculite, p 123
Viburnums, p 46
Vines, pp 49, 50
Virginia creeper, p 50

W

Watering, pp 37, 39, 58, 60, 74
Weeding knife, p 104
Weeds, pp 39, 72, 73, 121, 125
Weeping willow, p 82
Weigela, p 47
Wheelbarrow, p 103
Wheel hoe, p 106
White birch, p 85
White clover, p 32
Winter creeper, p 50
Wisteria, p 50

Y

Yew, p 9

Z

Zinnia, p 56